SLLA

Practice Questions

SLLA Practice Tests and Exam Review for the School Leaders Licensure Assessment

Dear Future Exam Success Story

First of all, **THANK YOU** for purchasing Mometrix study materials!

Second, congratulations! You are one of the few determined test-takers who are committed to doing whatever it takes to excel on your exam. **You have come to the right place.** We developed these practice tests with one goal in mind: to deliver you the best possible approximation of the questions you will see on test day.

Standardized testing is one of the biggest obstacles on your road to success, which only increases the importance of doing well in the high-pressure, high-stakes environment of test day. Your results on this test could have a significant impact on your future, and these practice tests will give you the repetitions you need to build your familiarity and confidence with the test content and format to help you achieve your full potential on test day.

Your success is our success

We would love to hear from you! If you would like to share the story of your exam success or if you have any questions or comments in regard to our products, please contact us at **800-673-8175** or **support@mometrix.com**.

Thanks again for your business and we wish you continued success!

Sincerely,
The Mometrix Test Preparation Team

Printed in the United States of America

TABLE OF CONTENTS

Practice Test #1

Selected-Response Questions

1. Which of these is true regarding school leader efforts involving school improvement plans, policies, and structures to improve parent engagement, student engagement, and student achievement?

a. School improvement plans increased parental meeting attendance but not student school attendance.
b. School improvement plans decreased student behavior problems while increasing their achievement.
c. Central office policies and structures increased parent engagement in individual schools, not systems.
d. School improvement plans increased student enrollment and achievement, not parent involvement.

2. Which of the following strategies for implementing technology is most closely related to leadership in implementing a school improvement plan?

a. Utilizing technology as a tool to facilitate collaboration among staff
b. Utilizing technology as a tool to administer assessments to students
c. Utilizing technology as a tool for communication among stakeholders
d. Utilizing technology as a tool to collect, organize, and analyze data for school improvement and progress monitoring

3. Challenges to school leaders for promoting student mental health include limited resources. Among such limitations, which is most related to federal accountability mandates?

a. Ratios of school counselors to students
b. School counselor responsibility change
c. Inadequate support staff development
d. Districts' mental health staff budgeting

4. Which of these is a valid guideline for school leaders to support staff throughout their professional development (PD)?

a. To be job-embedded and school-based, PD must occur in the school building.
b. For effective PD, teachers must not learn passively, but be actively involved.
c. Because teachers are the ones involved in PD, it should be teacher-centered.
d. PD must be done independently to ensure individual learning and growth.

5. Nationally, public-school districts receive the largest proportion of funding from which of the following sources?

a. Federal government
b. Their city government
c. The state government
d. Various other sources

6. A school leader unveiled the new school vision and goals for the academic year at a community meeting. Several parents and community members were not pleased with the presentation and were vocal in their opposition of the leader's plan. Which of the following was the most likely cause of poor community support for the school vision and goals?

a. The vision and goals were not aligned.
b. The goals were not rigorous enough to meet state and federal accountability standards.
c. Stakeholders were not included in the development of the vison and goals.
d. The community members do not support the school leader.

7. Alternative high school principals Mohr and Dichter (2001) codified developmental stages that school staff undergo to become learning communities. Which stage is associated with the emergence of a sense of community?

a. The stage involving conflict
b. The honeymoon stage
c. The confusion stage
d. The mature stage

8. A school leader wants to enlist support for change on campus. Which of the following actions should be taken first?

a. Communicate the intended change effectively to all stakeholders.
b. Create an advisory committee.
c. Find supporters with influence over other stakeholders to help spread the word about the change.
d. Administer an anonymous survey to see how stakeholders feel about the proposed change.

9. To evaluate teacher effectiveness in applying instructional strategies, school leaders need a working knowledge of student-centered, research-based teaching methods. What is most true about these?

a. The Socratic method is a useful, research-based strategy for delivering instruction.
b. Project-based learning requires technology integration in order to be implemented effectively.
c. Cooperative learning has been proven to be an effective, research-based instructional strategy.
d. It is necessary for teachers to utilize technology to deliver instruction in order to be effective.

10. Which of the following actions best demonstrates collaboration with teachers to maintain an instructional program that delivers standards-based instruction?

a. Audit instructional materials used in the classroom, including worksheets and teacher-developed materials.
b. Compare student course grades to performance on standardized tests.
c. Engage in professional learning communities with teachers to contribute to planning discussions about the curriculum.
d. Survey teachers to obtain feedback about new curriculum options.

11. School leadership experts have observed that many available forms of school data can be more significant for informing and guiding the school vision than the kinds of data educators tend to think of automatically. Which choice represents this default assumption that can exclude other valuable data?

a. Standardized achievement, state, local common, AP, and IB test results
b. Data that measure rates of student attendance, absence, and tardiness
c. Rates of attendance, absence, and turnover of grade or department staffs
d. Student extracurricular enrollments and incidents and dispositions in discipline

12. Which of the following is NOT true about the qualifications of teachers in public schools?

a. Teachers must be fully-certified to teach in a public school.
b. Teachers must be highly-qualified to teach in a public school.
c. A teacher who moves states may have to demonstrate subject-matter competency in the new state to teach.
d. Teachers in high-performing schools generally have more qualifications than teachers in other public schools.

13. Which of the following should school principals primarily look for when observing teachers in classrooms for evaluation purposes?

a. They should focus on what students want to learn rather than what they want them to learn.
b. They should look for how comfortable the teacher is with the lesson content and method of delivery.
c. They should look for evidence of learning such as student responses to checks for understanding and student work products.
d. They should focus on physical classroom setup.

14. Which instructional materials would most promote student reflection?

a. Textbook end-of-chapter study questions
b. Venn diagrams and other graphic organizers
c. Journals for students to write in regularly
d. Worksheets for exercising new learning

15. A goal for XYZ High School is to increase teachers' and students' technology skills. Which of the following decisions best demonstrates that the leader is aligning resources to achieve the goal?

a. Require all staff communications to be paperless.
b. Purchase updated computers for teachers and students and provide training for using them.
c. Conduct regular professional development for teachers related to technology skills.
d. Offer a new course to students that teaches basic computer skills.

16. The Individuals with Disabilities Education Act (IDEA) is a law that:

a. Requires teachers to be highly qualified
b. Ensures that all children with disabilities have free and appropriate education
c. Mandates that elementary schools have pre-kindergarten programs
d. Allows students with disabilities to be exempt from state and federal testing

17. The principal has noted that Mr. Smith, a star teacher, arrives late to school every day. The assistant principal who supervises Mr. Smith informs the principal that no one bothers Mr. Smith about his late arrival because he does such a great job in the classroom. The assistant principal's action is a violation of:

a. Fairness
b. Integrity
c. Justice
d. Trust

18. When schools and leaders implement the continuous school improvement process, which should they do *first*?

a. Establish specific goals for school improvements
b. Reflect on instructional and leadership practices
c. Implement strategies for specific improvements
d. Conduct needs assessments for their schools

19. How can a school and its leaders best control the quality of the teaching faculty?

a. Focus on retaining effective teachers to prevent having to recruit new teachers.
b. Focus on attracting, retaining, and developing effective teachers.
c. Focus on hiring and developing effective teachers rather than recruiting new teachers.
d. Focus on retaining quality teachers rather than firing ineffective teachers.

20. A school leader is looking to incorporate daily effort into professional development in a collaborative way across the campus. Which of the following professional development and learning opportunities is NOT collaborative in nature and useful for daily teacher activities?

a. Conducting action research
b. Professional learning communities (PLCs)
c. Daily reading of professional research in journal publications
d. Structured observations

21. A newly appointed principal has been advised that the teachers on campus are disgruntled and resistant to change. Which of the following is the best action for the principal to take first to address this issue?

a. Send out a survey to all teachers to assess campus culture.
b. Meet with a focus group of teacher leaders and allow them to voice their concerns.
c. Hold an all-staff meeting and communicate the vision for the school.
d. Send an email to all teachers informing them of new policies and procedures.

22. An elementary school principal serves at a school in which many of the parents of students speak little or no English. The language barrier creates challenges in communication, parent engagement, and the reinforcement of learning at home. Which of the following actions would best help the principal to address this challenge?

a. Hire a translator to communicate with parents.
b. Partner with an adult ESL program in the community and offer free ESL classes on campus.
c. Translate all school documents to the languages of the parents.
d. Ask students to translate information for their parents.

23. Which of the following is the most crucial question to consider when developing school goals?

a. Are the school goals based on accurate data?
b. Are the school goals achievable?
c. Are the school goals aligned with the school vision?
d. Were stakeholders given the opportunity to participate in the development of the school goals?

24. Which of the following is a practice of a school leader that facilitates family involvement in education?

a. Hiring parent facilitators using state Title I and Smart Start funds.
b. Working extended hours on campus.
c. Collaborating with parents who are already involved in school activities.
d. Sending an e-newsletter to parents weekly.

25. According to the federal government, the core components of a response strategy to information system threats and breaches are policy, plan, and procedure. Which of the following is a function of the policy component?

a. Defining staff responsibilities and mechanisms for remediation
b. Identifying needed management support and school resources
c. Standardizing response tasks and behaviors and averting errors
d. Conducting risk assessments on a regular basis as a preparation

26. Which of the following is true regarding best practices for school leaders when giving teachers observational feedback?

a. Leaders should give feedback statements rather than asking questions.
b. Leaders should disregard strengths to focus on improving weaknesses.
c. Leaders should emphasize all identified areas for improvement equally.
d. Leaders should include some specific next steps attainable for teachers.

27. Regarding how school leaders involve students appropriately in school improvement teams and processes, which of the following is true?

a. Planning school-wide forums is always a school leader's job
b. Some students have conducted school-wide survey research
c. Students have never participated in hiring any school leader
d. Students testifying in the state legislatures is against the law

28. Which of the following best represents transparent decision-making?

a. The principal meets with a focus group prior to making a decision.
b. The principal administers a survey and considers the data prior to making a decision.
c. The principal informs the community that a decision needs to be made about eliminating the dance program and shares data that may impact the decision.
d. The principal posts meeting minutes from committee meetings online.

29. Which of the following best defines equity?

a. Providing all students with the same amount of resources and support
b. Providing students with the resources and support that meet their individual needs
c. Providing at-risk students with additional resources and support
d. Providing accommodations for students who receive special education services

30. Which of the following is not accurate regarding school leaders' engagement of faculty and staff in ongoing self-assessment and improvement?

a. To encourage self-direction in improving, leaders should model self-assessment and improvement.
b. To encourage self-direction in improving, leaders should actively engage workers.
c. To encourage self-direction in improving, leaders should make learning accessible.
d. To encourage self-direction in improving, leaders should leave self-improvement up to employees.

31. Which pedagogical shift best supports the integration of technology into instructional practice?

a. From homogenous student groups to heterogenous student groups
b. From learning passively to learning actively
c. From teacher-directed learning to student-paced learning
d. From lesson activities to project-based learning

32. How should school leaders and others analyze school data to inform the school vision?

a. Across grade levels instead of across school years
b. By subject matter rather than by student cohorts
c. By formative and summative assessment findings
d. By teachers within grades instead of across levels

33. Which of the following best represents a mutually beneficial relationship between a school and a community organization?

a. A neighborhood grocery store donates bottled water to the basketball team for home games.
b. The school hosts a clothing drive for a local homeless shelter once a year.
c. A local church has permission to use the school library for meetings on Saturday mornings and the principal is permitted to make announcements to the attendees during the meetings.
d. A medical clinic near the school offers free immunizations and physicals to students actively enrolled at the school.

34. Which of the following accurately represents how school leaders can promote equitable access to curriculum for all students and their parents?

a. They can make staff more comfortable in discussing diversity without promoting equity.
b. They can clarify school staff misconceptions related to deficit theories about minorities.
c. They can model equity in daily interactions, but should avoid confronting discrimination.
d. They can create safe environments, though student support networks are not their job.

35. In school-wide positive behavior support (SPBS) programs, which of the following is a procedure associated with tier 3?

a. Socio-emotional groups
b. Daily check-in and check-out
c. Intervention family support
d. Individualized interventions

36. Relative to developing and sustaining a clear school vision and learning goals, which choice correctly describes documented practices of effective school principals?

a. They protect educators' instructional time via minimizing disruptions.
b. They set aspirational goals that they do not expect everyone to meet.
c. They have a clear vision for the school and always focus on one vision.
d. They ensure continual progress monitoring regardless of school goals.

37. Which of the following is the best way to identify strategies for facilitating change?

a. Host student and teacher focus groups to solicit suggestions and ideas.
b. Conduct pilot programs and collect data to determine efficacy.
c. Study research-based and proven best practices.
d. Meet with community stakeholders to solicit suggestions and ideas.

38. XYZ school district requires a minimum number of professional development hours to be completed by teachers employed in the district annually. A high school principal notices that each year, teachers have difficulty meeting this expectation and look for last minute professional development opportunities at the end of the school year. What action might the principal take to address this issue?

a. Personally deliver professional development sessions to staff monthly.
b. Allocate more money in the budget to professional development.
c. Monitor professional development activities more frequently throughout the school year.
d. Provide incentives to teachers who complete their professional development activities at the beginning of the school year.

39. Which of the following laws dictates how student information can be used in an educational setting?

a. HIPAA
b. FERPA
c. NCLB
d. ESSA

40. Which of the following practices by school leaders most effectively improves teacher practice and student learning?

a. Reviewing student performance data and sharing aggregated results with teachers
b. Administering self-assessment surveys to teachers
c. Conducting regular classroom observations and providing timely feedback
d. Offering educational resources to teachers related to their identified areas of weakness

41. Which of the following actions best demonstrates a middle school leader monitoring instructional practices and student progress to ensure that all students are prepared for a challenging curriculum?

a. Offering a summer bridge program for underperforming seventh-grade students entering eighth-grade.
b. Reviewing the performance of incoming sixth-grade students on standardized tests.
c. Evaluating the course grades of eighth-grade students enrolled in an Algebra I course for high school credit.
d. Comparing student performance on standardized tests to course grades to determine alignment of assessment.

42. Which of the following is the best example of differentiated instruction based on product?

a. Teach different content for different students.
b. Allow students to choose between writing an essay or recording a video for an assignment.
c. Give students different version of assessments.
d. Assign some students to watch a video while others read an article.

43. Which of the following is the least effective way that school leaders can create inclusive school communities?

a. Encourage students whose parents do not speak English to translate for them when interacting with school staff.
b. Provide video recordings and resources to parents who miss workshops and meetings.
c. Validate, honor, and thank family and community for supporting the school.
d. Hire parent liaisons to help parents access resources and services offered by the school.

44. Which of the following actions is NOT an example of a school leader functioning as an instrument of social justice?

a. Writing a letter to the State Board of Education regarding education funding
b. Participating in a community rally to protest the construction of a railroad through the neighborhood
c. Becoming a paid member of an education organization for urban school leaders
d. Campaigning in the school cafeteria for a political candidate in an upcoming election

45. Which of the following professional development activities would likely have the most impact on current teacher performance?

a. A self-paced book study program for all teachers
b. Online courses that teachers select and participate in at their own pace.
c. A four-hour in-person training conducted during the school year
d. A hybrid online and in-person six-week course that meets weekly for a cohort of teachers

46. During the annual summer meeting, the math department chair expresses concern that the math teachers do not have enough collaborative time to plan lessons and discuss student performance. Which of the following solutions would best address the department chair's concern?

a. Make adjustments to the master schedule to allot collaborative planning time for the math department.
b. Offer extra duty pay for math teachers to stay after school and plan together.
c. Purchase a technology platform that will allow the teachers to communicate asynchronously online.
d. Place substitute teachers in the math classrooms monthly to allow teachers time to plan together.

47. Which of the following most accurately reflects how school leaders can identify and decrease educational and institutional bias and discriminatory practices?

a. Establish anti-discrimination rules and identify a campus leader to enforce them.
b. Establish an anti-discrimination policy and form a committee to find opportunities to learn about and promote other cultures.
c. Hire a culturally diverse leadership team and have them speak to staff and students about their cultures.
d. Include opportunities in the curriculum for students to learn about other cultures.

48. A female member of a school's staff sends a letter to the principal. Her complaint is that her supervisor, who is male, calls her and other female employees by names such as "dear", "honey," and so on. The writer of the letter perceives this as disrespectful. In following up, the principal discovers the content of the complaint is confirmed as fact but also that the majority of the rest of the female staff do not perceive the male supervisor as disrespectful in his forms of address. Which action regarding the complaint would be most appropriate?

a. Telling the letter writer that other females on the school staff do not agree with her about the names.
b. Telling the supervisor that some staff are offended, and that referring to female employees in this manner is unprofessional.
c. Calling a meeting of female school staff and their supervisor to review laws on workplace sexual harassment.
d. Calling a meeting with the supervisor to reprimand him and ask him to make a public apology to staff.

49. Which of the following is most effective in motivating members of the educational community when implementing new policies?

a. Delegating authority to staff members
b. Communicating unexpected barriers to the community as they arise
c. Sharing the policies frequently using a variety of communication channels
d. Including stakeholders in the development of new policies

Refer to the following for question 50:

A new school principal administered a survey to school staff to assess the perceived culture of the school. The data from the survey showed that most of the staff felt that all ideas for the school came from the top and were forced down. The school principal wants to shift the culture and encourage staff to be innovative.

50. Of the following, how could the school principal best provide a safe environment for teachers to express their beliefs and ideas to help them feel more involved?

a. Schedule monthly one-on-one meetings with individual teachers.
b. Place a suggestion box in the teachers' lounge.
c. Administer an electronic survey to campus staff to obtain feedback.
d. Provide collaborative meeting time for teachers and meet with them regularly to discuss their ideas.

51. Of the following, which accurately reflects a principle of adult learning that applies to professional development (PD) for teachers?

a. Adults learn best when participation in PD is required.
b. Adults learn best when learning materials are selected and provided.
c. Adults learn best when they are involved in planning the instruction.
d. Adults learn best when informed about how they will be assessed prior to participation.

52. A school leader wants to create a risk-taking environment for teachers where they feel comfortable improving their practices for teaching and learning. Which of the following actions should the school leader take to accomplish this goal?

a. Create a system of peer evaluations.
b. Allow teachers to choose their own professional development opportunities.
c. Create a digital data dashboard so teachers can share achievement data with one another.
d. Place a suggestion box in the teachers' lounge.

53. Which of the following would be most likely to cause an administrator to look for outside resources in assisting students and their families?

a. A student is having difficulty in math class.
b. Two students participated in a physical altercation.
c. A student and his or her family are struggling financially and are in need of food and clothing.
d. A student will be the first in the family to graduate high school.

54. The campus technology coordinator recommends to the principal that new desktop computers be purchased for three of the campus's computer labs. The dean of instruction recommends that classroom technology should be upgraded first. Which of the following strategies should the principal implement first to decide how to prioritize these recommendations in the school's technology budget?

a. The principal should physically inspect the current equipment to determine which is in the most need of replacement.
b. The principal should refer to the campus improvement plan to determine how the recommendations align with the vision and goals for the school.
c. The principal should seek donations from stakeholders to assist with improving technology across the campus.
d. The principal should determine which of the recommendations is most economical.

55. Which of the following principles about formative assessment should school leaders consider when giving feedback to and collaborating with teachers?

a. Student motivation and learning are unaffected by assessment types.
b. Student motivation and learning are affected by assessment types.
c. Error is inevitable in all assessment, and only summative assessment is a valid indicator of student learning.
d. Student performance against a standard is more important than student growth.

56. When developing a vision for the school, which of the following sources of information is most critical to consider?

a. School, local, state, and federal policies
b. Past school performance indicators
c. Feedback from students, staff, and other stakeholders
d. Performance of similar schools

57. At a PTA meeting, a concerned community member stated that there were no programs offered at the high school that prepared students for jobs in the community and that there was too much focus on sending students to college. Which of the following best describes the action that the principal can take to address the community member's concern?

a. Inform the community member that preparing students for college is the school's primary responsibility.
b. Promise the community member that course offerings will be revised for the upcoming school year.
c. Ask the community member which jobs in the community the school should prepare students for.
d. Collect and review employment trend data in the community to determine if school course offerings need to be revised to meet community needs.

58. What must school leaders consider to mobilize and develop community school support?

a. Businesses and community-based organizations use the same language that educators use.
b. Exchanging and matching visions, missions, wants, and needs with stakeholders is sufficient.
c. Prospective community partners primarily want to know how collaboration benefits schools.
d. Prospective partner motivations are as varied as the organizations interested in partnership.

59. Experts find that, to build community capacity for contributing to school improvement, school leaders and staff must transcend traditional activities. What is true about how they can further continue community collaboration for school improvement?

a. For productive partnerships, schools should give stakeholders information only as they request it.
b. School leaders and staff should identify which community members can participate meaningfully.
c. All collaborations with community members should align directly with the campus vision and goals.
d. To engage and retain community partners, schools should limit the achievement data they share.

60. A school leader wants to become more involved in analyzing student work on campus. Which of the following actions should the school leader take to accomplish this goal?

a. Audit student work samples and discuss the student performance demonstrated with the teachers who assigned the work.
b. Monitor teacher grade books.
c. Host a science fair.
d. Mandate that teachers assess student learning using portfolios.

61. Which of the following actions best demonstrates that a principal makes decisions to improve instruction based on evidence from student data?

a. Meeting with parents frequently during grading periods
b. Conducting meetings for Professional Learning Committees based on grade levels and subject areas
c. Requiring teachers to host tutorial sessions for students after the regular school day
d. Submitting reports to district office personnel after each grading period

62. A school leader is developing school goals for the campus for the new academic school year. Which of the following should be included in the goals to best support a culture of learning?

a. Increased student attendance rates
b. Improved teacher evaluation ratings
c. Decreased student dropout rate
d. Increased student completion of advanced placement courses

63. Which of the following is accurate about the uses of data in goal-related activities?

a. Qualitative data is not useful when setting goals aligned with school vision and mission.
b. Data connected to vision and mission enable monitoring progress for goals.
c. Only formative data is relevant to how schools allocate resources to meet their goals.
d. Formal data collection is not necessary to assess family and community relations.

64. A high school principal is concerned that ninth-grade students who read below grade level are not performing well on benchmark tests in reading and writing. Which of the following steps should the principal take to best address this concern?

a. Provide test preparation sessions for these students after school and on weekends and monitor student attendance to the sessions.
b. Integrate reading and writing skills into all subject areas and provide training to all teachers on fundamental reading strategies.
c. Increase the opportunities that students have to spend in the school library.
d. Purchase a reading software program that students can use at home.

65. Which of the following statements is most accurate about how school leaders align school policies and practices with federal, state, district, and local school system policies?

a. State standardized assessment instruments are based solely on standards developed by states.
b. Individual schools directly apply state standards for developing their standardized assessments.
c. Schools directly reflect system standards, and yet ultimately are also aligned with federal policy.
d. Local school districts develop standardized assessments applying the federal standards directly.

66. In public school districts, which personnel are *not* likely to be directly supervised by the campus principal?

a. Bus drivers
b. Custodians
c. Volunteers
d. Cafeteria workers

67. A dean of instruction of a middle school wants to increase the number and variety of resources that teachers have access to. Which of the following actions should the dean take to accomplish this goal?

a. Encourage teachers to purchase instructional resources and provide reimbursement for their expenses.
b. Survey teachers to identify which resources they would like to have and purchase resources from their suggestions.
c. Provide teachers with asynchronous, on-demand professional development sessions online.
d. Seek free and discounted resources from vendors in the local area.

68. Which of the following is an effective way to use community resources to support student learning?

a. Invite local churches to host a back-to-school drive to provide students with school supplies.
b. Partner with local businesses to provide free tutoring to students after school.
c. Partner with local businesses to host field trips for students.
d. Invite local businesspersons in the community to mentor students.

69. Which of the following statements is most accurate about why schools must collaborate with their communities in providing mental health services to remove learning barriers and improve student outcomes?

a. In many communities and states, schools are often children's only mental health service providers.
b. Due to stigma associated with mental health needs, parents avoid familiar school settings and staff.
c. According to research study findings, students are less likely to seek counseling services in schools.
d. Mental health services in schools should be separated from mental health services in communities.

70. A school leader is faced with an impending budget cut for the upcoming school year. When deciding how to reallocate funds, which of the following strategies should the school leader implement?

a. Identify the most expensive budget items and reduce their allocations.
b. Identify the least expensive budget items and eliminate them.
c. Prioritize budget items that most closely align to the school goals.
d. Apply for grants to replace the lost funds.

71. Which is a practice that national research studies find school leaders should *avoid* when speaking publicly and in other communication with key stakeholders?

a. Taking advantage of the political environment
b. Using commonly understood language with most audiences
c. Communicating in response to sensitive situations
d. Becoming engaged in large scale open forums

72. A math intervention program that was implemented on a high school campus for the previous school year was funded by a grant that is expired. The principal must determine whether to fund the program using the local budget or to eliminate the program. Which of the following data points would best inform the principal as to whether the math intervention program should continue to be funded?

a. Student attendance in the program
b. Feedback from students regarding the program
c. Student math performance data from the beginning of the school year compared to the end of the school year
d. Student performance on the state mandated assessment for the previous school year

73. A school principal has decided to partner with a local community center to provide a basketball camp for students after school. The camp is free to students and the school will not pay the community center any funds for hosting the camp. Based on this agreement, what should the principal do next?

a. Begin recruiting students for the camp.
b. Draft a memorandum of understanding for both parties to sign.
c. Send an email to the director of the community center reiterating the arrangement that was agreed upon.
d. Find an organization that offers a football camp for students who do not want to play basketball.

74. Among classroom assessment principles that school leaders must know for effective collaboration with teachers, which choice is MOST representative?

a. A few specific assessment instruments are error free.
b. Authors and users typically overestimate testing error.
c. Assessment reliability applies to tests, not test scores.
d. Good assessment is valid, reliable, ethical, and fair.

Refer to the following for question 75:

The school principal reviews classroom observation and feedback with assistant principals weekly but often has very few classroom observations of their own conducted in preparation for the weekly meeting. This week, a teacher complained to the principal that the feedback from their most recent evaluation was not fair because it did not provide a well-rounded view of their performance.

75. What action should the school principal take to increase the frequency of classroom visits?

a. Make a commitment to visit classrooms every morning before the day gets too busy.
b. Clear their schedule on a specific day of the week to dedicate to classroom visits.
c. Plan out the classrooms that should be visited for the week and add them to the calendar with reminders.
d. Carry classroom observation forms at all times and visit classrooms when an opportunity presents itself.

76. Among challenges that school leaders face in their efforts to promote student mental health, which of the following descriptions most represents the category of limited resources?

a. Accountability law has shifted school counselors' duties from mental health to academic achievement.
b. Prevention and promotion can address most student issues, yet costly treatments are routinely prescribed.
c. The mental health resources available to public schools are not provided proportionately or equitably.
d. Owing to our society's cultural traditions, the priority of mental health issues in schools is marginalized.

77. In many public-school districts, students with certain linguistic and/or cultural backgrounds are disproportionately enrolled in special education programs. How can a school leader best address this type of overrepresentation?

a. Examine current school procedures for assigning grade levels to students.
b. Examine instructional strategies targeting students referred to special education.
c. Examine instruments used to evaluate student need for special education.
d. Examine the curriculum and related expectations of student achievement.

78. The research literature about school principals' roles in realizing the school vision and goals, and aligning instruction with the vision and goals, affords which of these conclusions?

a. Principals with more effective schools focus on learning rather than on school improvement.
b. Principals with high-achieving schools have more confidence in teachers than in themselves.
c. Principals with effective schools delegate the roles of assuring instructional quality to others.
d. Principals with high-achieving schools communicate to all stakeholders that learning comes first.

79. What do psychologists recommend regarding tiered models of student behavior management in education?

a. Tiered models of behavior management work only with school-wide behavior support systems.
b. Tiered models of behavior management are most effective when addressing individual disruptive student behavior.
c. Tiered models of behavior management are most applicable for classroom or school-wide implementation.
d. Tiered models of behavior management are judged best for individuals, classrooms, or schools.

80. The PTO president expressed concern to the school principal about the recent announcement to purchase new science curriculum for ninth and tenth-grade students. He expressed that there was a greater need for college preparation materials for students. Which of the following responses from the principal is best?

a. Purchasing science curriculum was the economic choice because it will benefit a greater number of students for a smaller cost.
b. College preparation materials will be considered for purchase for the upcoming school year.
c. Student performance data demonstrates that students are already performing at a satisfactory level on college entrance exams.
d. One of the school goals for the year is to improve student performance in science and the curriculum purchase supports that goal.

81. Which of the following represents a potential conflict of interest?

a. A potential contractor for remodeling the gymnasium is a relative of the school principal.
b. The assistant principal's son attends the school where he or she works.
c. The principal owns a house in the community that the school serves.
d. The math software that the district adopted was used in a school district where the principal served prior.

82. Which of the following best describes school leader responsibilities related to school safety policies?

a. Leaders must ensure school safety policies comply with federal laws only.
b. Leaders must notify staff and parents in advance of any changes affecting safety or health.
c. Leaders are solely responsible for developing and revising safety policies.
d. Leaders do not have the responsibility of warning parents about environmental hazards.

83. Which of the following informs how school leaders can incorporate diverse family and community aspirations and expectations into their educational decision-making and planning?

a. Family aspirations for children vary markedly by culture.
b. Ethnicity strongly influences family academic aspiration.
c. Income affects family expectations more than race does.
d. Studies find high family aspirations across demographics.

84. To submit a budget to the school district office, a school leader must specify what resources the school will need to administer toward its instructional program for English language learner (ELL) students in the coming fiscal year. What should the leader's initial step be?

a. Identifying the percentage of district funds allocated in the last fiscal year for the ELL program
b. Identifying federal and state program requirements and basing resource calculations on these
c. Projecting resource amounts required for maintaining other school programs' current funding
d. Evaluating the effectiveness of the school ELL instructional program for students participating

85. School emergency response team organization is modeled after the Incident Command System (ICS) of Homeland Security's National Incident Management System (NIMS). Main ICS functions include Finance. Which of the ICS Management Systems identifies services and resources to support incident response needs?

a. Logistics
b. Planning
c. Command
d. Operations

86. Which of the following is most accurate about effective and appropriate school and co-curricular activities to prepare high school students for college and careers?

a. Career and technical education can only be obtained in magnet or technical schools.
b. School partnerships with higher education institutions best prepare students for jobs.
c. Community-based and project-based learning prepare students for higher education.
d. High school curricula should be pertinent to student lives, communities, and cultures.

87. Which of the following would provide the most valid indication of a culture of high expectations?

a. Setting campus goals above minimum standards
b. Hosting award ceremonies for high-achieving students
c. Recognizing the Teacher of the Year publicly
d. Holding regular community meetings to discuss school performance with stakeholders

88. What correctly represents National Education Association (NEA) guidelines for school acceptable use policies (AUPs) regarding classroom Internet technology?

a. It should have a policy statement including covered computer services and student use conditions.
b. It should have a definition section covering important terms used, but a preamble is not necessary.
c. It should include a section that defines acceptable use, but not one that defines unacceptable use.
d. It should include a violations or sanctions section, which should only define violations of the policy.

89. Which of the following is correct about effective classroom management systems?

a. Tiered positive behavior support models provide both prevention and intervention.
b. Tiered positive behavior support models are only for preventing behavior problems.
c. Tiered positive behavior support models are designed to be behavior interventions.
d. Tiered positive behavior support models provide less time in academic engagement.

90. Which of the following most correctly represents criteria requiring a school to hold a Manifestation Determination Review for a student who receives special education services?

a. The school seeks a discipline-related placement change for more than 10 days in a row.
b. The school suspends a student on a one-time basis for 10 or fewer consecutive days.
c. The school suspends a student for 10 or more days in a school year for any reason.
d. The school creates or revises a behavior intervention plan.

91. A community group has requested the use of the school gymnasium for an upcoming event. Which of the following should the principal consider first before approving the request?

a. Whether the group has a religious affiliation
b. Whether the request is in accordance with school and district policy for use of school facilities
c. Whether the event occurs during the school day
d. The fee that should be charged for rental of the gymnasium

92. Of the following, which is an advantage of developing a school vision collaboratively?

a. Visions developed through collaboration can be implemented far faster.
b. Visions are clearer and more coherent when developed by collaboration.
c. Visions take longer times in the process of development, slowing change.
d. Visions tend to be more appropriate to their local school district contexts.

93. Which of the following is the best example of a school leader utilizing technology to support effective school organization management?

a. Using technology to reconcile the budget and coordinate facility operations
b. Using technology to text message and email stakeholders about meetings
c. Using technology to collect, disaggregate, and analyze different school data
d. Using technology to facilitate multiple stakeholder contributions to projects

94. Staff morale at ABC Elementary school is very low and is impacting staff and student performance. Which of the following steps should the principal take first to repair staff morale?

a. Host an all-staff pep rally to encourage everyone.
b. Create a committee to advise the principal on how to repair staff morale.
c. Buy gifts for the staff.
d. Administer a survey to identify the causes of low morale.

95. A doctor who has a clinic in the community informs the principal that she is willing to provide free physicals to students at the school who would like to participate in athletics. How should the principal respond?

a. Decline the offer because students are responsible for getting physicals completed on their own.
b. Decline the offer if it cannot apply to the entire student body.
c. Accept the offer and create a log to document students who take advantage of the free physical.
d. Accept the offer only if the doctor can complete the physicals on campus after school hours.

96. Which of the following criteria would make a school the best candidate for implementing an integrated management system as new technology for managing school operations?

a. The school has not been using any digital management system.
b. The school has been using one management system with no plans for more.
c. The school has one or more systems and plans on adding more systems.
d. The school wants separate system policies and documentation.

97. The dean of instruction conducted a classroom observation of a seventh-grade math teacher and noticed that the math teacher was not following the curriculum for the math department. When asked, the math teacher informed the dean that the students were not ready for the standards identified in the curriculum and that he chose to review standards from sixth- grade instead.

Which of the following would be the best response from the dean to the math teacher?

a. Commend the math teacher for addressing the gaps in student learning.
b. Require that the math teacher attend training on the math curriculum.
c. Model instruction of the standards outlined in the curriculum.
d. Direct the math teacher to teach the standards outlined in the curriculum.

98. Which of the following strategies would most likely encourage stakeholders to support and implement the school vision and goals?

a. Announcing the school vision and goals at a community meeting.
b. Publishing the school vision and goals on the school website.
c. Including internal and external community members in the development of the vision and goals.
d. Selecting representatives from the staff and community to be advocates for the school's vision and goals.

99. In reference to the Supportive School Discipline Initiative (SSDI), former US Attorney General Eric Holder said a federal initiative to guide school disciplinary practices would "make schools safe, supportive and inclusive for all students" and would "keep America's young people safe and on the right path." How did he say it would do these things?

a. By making discipline less exclusionary
b. By divorcing discipline from civil rights
c. By getting data from resource officers
d. By referring discipline to peace officers

100. According to the National School Boards Association (NSBA), which of the following reflects an unintended consequence of the Healthy, Hunger-Free Kids Act (2010)?

a. School districts are not committed to giving students healthy nutrition.
b. Many school districts cannot afford the higher costs of new standards.
c. This legislation provides all funding for compliance with its regulations.
d. Students are going hungry because the regulations limit food amounts.

101. The sixth-grade math department meets as a professional learning community and determines that overall students in sixth-grade are not performing well on the same three math objectives. However, these same students are performing satisfactorily on other math objectives. Which of the following is the most likely reason that the sixth-grade students are not mastering the identified math objectives?

a. The math teachers are ineffective in teaching the identified math objectives.
b. The curriculum is not properly aligned to address the identified math objectives.
c. The students need additional tutoring to master the identified math objectives.
d. The assessment used to measure student performance was biased.

102. Which of the following is most used in self-assessment to facilitate professional development?

a. Teachers write in journals about their work
b. Teachers apply advice they receive to work
c. Teachers analyze videos of their instruction
d. Teachers benefit from others' experiences

103. Which of the following strategies most accurately identifies the school leader's role in implementing professional development?

a. Staff development is the sole responsibility of the school leader.
b. A school leader should delegate the implementation of professional development to the administrative team.
c. A school leader should leverage teacher leaders in the implementation of professional development.
d. School leaders are directly responsible for implementing professional development but should utilize their administrative team and teacher leaders where appropriate.

104. To assist teachers with integrating technology into instruction, which should school leaders do?

a. Lead teachers first to encourage student technology use for enhancing research skills.
b. Lead teachers to avoid legal and ethical issues with technology as outside their scope.
c. Lead teachers to encourage student concept comprehension before using technology.
d. Lead teachers to target technology skills and content quality without differentiation.

105. A middle school principal decides to select and train several lead teachers in the math department to conduct action research on campus. This decision is an example of which of the following strategies?

a. Providing teachers with the opportunity to take appropriate risks for improving teaching and learning
b. Encouraging collaboration between teachers to support professional growth
c. Using data-driven decision making to improve student performance
d. Giving teachers a voice in school decisions

106. Which of the following is true about proactive strategies that successful school leaders have used to overcome resistance to change by school staff, families, communities, and school districts?

a. People fear change irrespective of school leader commitment.
b. Administrative support networks enhance change acceptance.
c. Establishing priorities tends to strengthen resistance to change.
d. How school leaders communicate has no impact on resistance.

107. Which of the following describes the school district policy to allow principals autonomy to spend their campus budget as they see fit?

a. Local school management
b. Hybrid financial decision-making
c. Budgetary autonomy
d. Decentralization

108. Which choice accurately reflects the school leader's role regarding laws protecting student rights to privacy and confidentiality of their educational records?

a. School leaders are responsible for knowing these rights but not enforcing them.
b. School leaders are responsible to enforce these but need not know exceptions.
c. School leaders are responsible for third-party disclosure but not written consent.
d. School leaders are responsible for policy on non-student and parent records access.

109. Which of the following is the most critical question to consider when using community resources in the classroom?

a. Are the resources aligned with the curriculum?
b. Are there enough resources for all students?
c. Are teachers familiar with these resources?
d. Are the resources expected to be returned?

110. What should school leaders keep in mind when integrating technology into standards-based curricula?

a. They should assign their teachers to write technology standards.
b. They cannot help students meet standards by using technology.
c. They do not need to require students to master technology standards.
d. They should focus on learning with technology, not learning about it.

111. What have researchers found regarding the relationship between student academic self-concepts and student outcomes?

a. Students' academic self-concepts are correlated with success later in life.
b. Students' academic self-concepts are correlated with their academic achievement.
c. Students' academic self-concepts are correlated with socioeconomic status more than home settings.
d. Students' academic self-concepts are correlated with enrollment in smaller schools.

112. According to multiple research studies, what is a characteristic of school leaders related to evaluating teacher effectiveness?

a. The most effective school leaders are better at identifying the best candidates for hiring as teachers.
b. The most effective school leaders are better at identifying the best and worst teachers on their staff.
c. The most effective teachers are attracted to the schools whose leaders have hired the best teachers.
d. The most effective school leaders are better at identifying excellent and average teachers than poorer ones.

113. According to research related to the factors that contribute to the success of higher-performing public schools, which of the following is true?

a. The school leader is the single defining success factor.
b. School success is based on a complex set of interrelated factors.
c. Schools cannot be successful without additional funding.
d. Factors related to curriculum and instruction are the most important determinants of success.

114. Which of the following is the best description of a transactional leader?

a. Willing to purchase new equipment to improve the current system
b. Works to change the culture by implementing new policies
c. Pursues efficiency in the school system through strong supervision
d. Seeks staff and community involvement in developing new ideas

Refer to the following for question 115:

A new school principal administered a survey to school staff to assess the perceived culture of the school. The data from the survey showed that most of the staff felt that all ideas for the school came from the top and were forced down. The school principal wants to shift the culture and encourage staff to be innovative.

115. Which of the following strategies would best help the principal to meet this goal?

a. Create action committees made up of teachers and staff and give the committees time and resources to generate solutions to campus needs.
b. Place a suggestion box in the teachers' lounge and encourage teachers to submit their ideas for consideration.
c. Inform the staff that there are positions on the Shared Decision-Making Committee for teachers and that they would feel more represented if they engaged in the process.
d. Host a town hall meeting and allow participants to share their ideas publicly.

116. In which of the following situations can family and community stakeholders be most helpful?

a. Identifying internships for students
b. Evaluating teacher performance
c. Analyzing student data
d. Conducting teacher training

117. To address inherent barriers like staff fear of the unknown and resistance to change, school principals benefit from knowing common kinds of inner dialogues employees experience around school vision development. What do school personnel typically ask themselves about this change process?

a. Not what is needed for the vision but if they will be able to live with and support it
b. If they believe they and the school can realize the vision rather than if they personally believe in it
c. Whether they will be able to continue their instructional practices, and why or why not
d. What the vision will expect and how their lives will change, as opposed to just practice continuity

118. Which of the following barriers would interfere the most with achieving a goal of increased student achievement in math?

a. A shortage of calculators
b. A lack of community support
c. The adoption of a new math textbook
d. The unexpected resignation of a math teacher

119. Which of the following accurately reflects evaluative criteria that school leaders should consider first when deciding to utilize community resources to support student learning?

a. Congruence with the school's vision and mission
b. Immediate impact on student achievement
c. Results from prior implementation
d. The relationship of the person or organization to the school

120. Who typically makes student enrollment projections for determining school budgets?

a. District Offices of Achievement and Accountability alone project the student enrollments
b. District Offices of Achievement and Accountability with school leader revision as needed
c. The school leader alone projects the student enrollments for his or her school every year
d. Final projections are by committees from the district finance and student support offices

Constructed Response

1. You are the principal of a school that historically was majority white, non-Hispanic/Latino, non-bilingual. Over the last ten years, the geographical area and your school has experienced a profound change in its demographic makeup. This school year 75% of the student body is Hispanic/Latino, 25% is white (non-Hispanic), and a large number of these are English Language Learners/Bilingual students. The staff of the school is predominately white, not bilingual, and has largely remained unchanged in ethnic makeup from previous year. A significant number of parents have become increasingly upset by what they perceive as a major communication barrier between parents, students, and school teachers/staff. The district superintendent has asked you to develop a new cultural competency program aimed at solving this problem. In 300-600 words, outline the program you would come up with. Include how the program would be implemented and whom the program would include.

2. You are the principal of a large suburban high school with a diverse student and teacher population. One day you overhear a group of students discussing one of their classmates and her relationship with the chemistry teacher, Mr. Bolyn. The students are debating if their classmate and Mr. Bolyn have had sexual relations yet or not. In 150-300 words, explain how you would address this situation.

3. You are starting your first year as principal at Mendoza High School, which has a diverse student population of about 1,500 students. Over the past several years the pass rate on the state mandated English exam has been declining and is now notably lower than the pass rate in other area high schools. Last school year (prior to your beginning at the school) the English department in conjunction with the faculty audited the school's curriculum and adjusted it to align with the state standards. This year, the superintendent has told you that you will have an additional $12,000 in discretionary funds to support the initiative to increase the pass rate of the English exam. In 300-600 words, outline two important issues you should consider when preparing recommendations for the discretionary budget, explain one strategy you can use to determine budget allocations to recommend that will promote improved student performance, and explain why the strategy you have described will likely be effective.

4. You are the principal of a 900-student middle school (6-8). The school recently formulated a school vision, which includes a critical goal of improving the academic and social-emotional preparedness of the school's eighth-graders for the transition to high school. Over the past several years, teachers and administrators in the local high school have become increasingly concerned about the level of preparedness of incoming ninth-grade students, who have been increasingly socially immature and lacking in vital academic and study skills. Various stakeholders (parents, students, teachers in both schools) attribute the problem to different reasons and would prescribe different remedies. You form a committee to improve the transition to high school for the eighth-graders in your school. Committee members include teachers, parents, student supports (social worker, school psychologist), a special education representative, and a curriculum coordinator.

Write a 150-300 word memo to the members of the committee about the plan to improve eighth-grade readiness for high school. Before you write the memo, state what assumptions you make about the school/community (rural/urban, demographics, socioeconomics). In the memo convey why you believe it is important for the school to succeed in this endeavor (improving preparedness for high school) and describe 2-3 significant aspects of the school's instructional program that the committee will address in developing its plan. For each of these specific aspects/factors describe a type of data or other information that the team should analyze and explain why this type of information may be useful in analyzing the specific area of concern.

Answer Key and Explanations for Test #1

Selected-Response Questions

1. B: School improvement plans have been found to increase parental meeting and student school attendance; student enrollment and achievement; parental involvement in policies, procedures, advocacy, organizing, and events; and to decrease student behavior problems while increasing student achievement. School system leaders have also established central office policies and structures that increased parental engagement, not only in individual schools but also system-wide.

2. D: A primary aspect of implementing a school improvement plan is to use data to assess goal progress and completion. Integrating technology tools to accomplish this can improve the ease at which school improvement progress can be measured and improve the timeliness and accuracy of response to progress checks. Utilizing technology in other areas such as to facilitate collaboration, administer assessments, and communicate with stakeholders are valuable; however, utilizing technology to collect, organize, and analyze data for school improvement and progress monitoring is most closely related to the implementation of the school improvement plan.

3. B: Among resource limitations, inadequate school counselor-to-student ratios are attributable to funding and budget cuts, not accountability mandates. Inadequate in-service development for new support staff is attributable to various factors, including cultural influences stigmatizing mental health issues, lowering their priority in schools; leadership and organizational deficits; and funding deficits, ineffective resource allocation, etc.—not accountability mandates. Inadequate school district mental health budgeting is not federally mandated for accountability. Federal accountability requirements have changed school counselor responsibilities from addressing student mental health to addressing student academic achievement, reducing professional support services.

4. B: Although professional development (PD) must be job-embedded and school-based, it can occur even outside of the school building if teachers view it as part of their daily work duties and it emerges from and contributes to daily classroom practice. Teachers must be actively involved in the learning process for effective PD. It should be student-centered so that teachers learn to support student learning because PD is not for teachers' own sake. Collaborative teacher problem-solving is a PD guideline because it is valuable, addresses the issue of teacher isolation, and fosters professional and community respect.

5. C: Allowing for variations across states, most public-school districts receive the largest proportion of funding from their state governments. According to the American Association of School Administrators (AASA), the federal government provides between 10 and 20 percent of the funding public school districts receive. Local and intermediate governments combined contributing slightly less than the state government. Only a very small proportion of funding comes from other sources.

6. C: It is important to involve stakeholders in the development of the school vision to help incorporate their varied perspectives into the vision and to increase buy in for the vision. Without buy in, community members and stakeholders may oppose the school vision and withdraw their support and resources for the school and school leadership.

7. B: Alternative high school principals (Mohr and Dichter, 2001) identified staff developmental stages of honeymoon, conflict, confusion, messy, scary, and mature, in that order, in becoming learning communities. The honeymoon stage is identified as when a sense of community first emerges. The conflict stage is summarized as "the honeymoon is over." The confusion stage is characterized by staff uncertainty over the leader's role. The messy stage involves increased lack of clarity. The scary stage finds staff wondering where accountability and authority are. The mature stage equates to the birth of a learning community.

8. A: Leaders intent on fostering change are required to strategically communicate the intended change and gather supporters for that change. First, the leader needs to communicate the intended change effectively. Many people are unwilling to support changes because they fear the unknown. The leader should communicate not only what is to be changed but also how the changes affect the various staff members and how the changes are aligned to the school vision and goals.

9. C: Cooperative learning, the process of facilitating student collaboration, develops social skills, teamwork, individual and collective responsibility, and group interdependence. The Socratic method is useful for facilitating student engagement, assessing student learning, and fostering critical thinking, but is not useful for delivering instruction. Project-based learning is useful for active, hands-on learning experiences and does not require technology to be implemented effectively. Technology is a useful tool for delivering instruction, but is not required; technology is also effective when students utilize technology to engage in the learning process, making technology more student-centered.

10. C: Collaboration requires that the school leader engage directly with teachers to maintain an instructional program that delivers standards-based instruction. PLCs are excellent opportunities to listen and provide input during the planning stage for delivering instruction. Auditing classroom materials and analyzing the accuracy of grading are good tools for evaluating the delivery of standards-based instruction but are not collaborative. Administering a survey about new curriculum is not collaborative and does not help to support implementation of current materials.

11. A: Experts observe educators often assume "data" simply mean test results (A). They point out school vision oversight teams and faculty should also review other available data significant for informing school vision, including student attendance, absence, and tardiness data (B); rates of staff attendance, absence—including most frequent days—grade-level and department staff absenteeism, and turnover rates (C); student enrollments in extracurricular activities (clubs, sports, etc.); disciplinary incidents—including referral types, referring departments, teams, and teachers—and dispositions, including detention, in-school suspension, suspension, and expulsion (D).

12. A: In some states, teachers do not have to be fully certified to teach in a public school. Teachers who are new to the profession and may be enrolled in an alternative teacher certification program may be allowed to teach in a public school on a probationary status. However, all teachers must demonstrate subject-matter competency prior to being deemed highly qualified and able to teach in a public school. States may vary in their requirements for teacher certification; therefore, a teacher who is highly qualified in one state may have to meet additional qualifications if they move to another state.

13. C: School principals should look for evidence of learning when conducting a classroom observation. Students should be given opportunities to respond and demonstrate learning throughout the lesson so that the teacher and the observer can determine whether students are learning the content. These opportunities may occur as questioning strategies, discussion, or through guided and independent practice. It is important for teachers to be comfortable with the instructional content and method of delivery, but this is not a primary focus of a classroom observation as a novice teacher can be nervous yet still effective. Additionally, the physical classroom setup should be conducive to learning but is not the primary focus of a classroom observation.

14. C: Study questions at the ends of textbook chapters typically help students recall or identify, locate, interpret, and apply information they just read more than reflect. Graphic organizers help students visualize and organize verbal, numerical, and abstract information. Worksheets help students practice what they have just learned. Writing regularly in journals promotes and gives students a method for reflection.

15. B: The goal is for both teachers and students to improve their computer skills; providing training to teachers or a new course for students does not fully address the school goal. Purchasing updated computers for students and teachers and training them to use the devices best demonstrates that the leader is using school resources to support the school goal.

16. B: The Individuals with Disabilities Education Act (IDEA) is a law that makes a free, appropriate, public education available to eligible children with disabilities throughout the nation and ensures special education and related services will be provided for those children. This law governs how states and public agencies provide educational services to children with disabilities. Congress reauthorized the IDEA in 2004 and most recently amended it through Public Law 114-95, the Every Student Succeeds Act, in December 2015 (US Department of Education).

17. A: Mr. Smith's performance in the classroom does not excuse him from meeting other professional expectations. The assistant principal's response implies that Mr. Smith would be held accountable for his late arrival if he were not doing a good job in the classroom. It is unfair to allow Mr. Smith to arrive late without allowing other teachers to do the same. Integrity is most often applied to situations of morality, while justice is most often applied to situations in which the appropriateness of consequences is questioned. In this scenario, it is implied that the violation of policy for arrival time is based upon teaching performance, which would indicate that teachers who do not perform as well may be held to strict adherence to the policy. There is no discussion of morality or administered consequences in this scenario, only the unequal application of the policy.

18. D: In a cycle of continuous school improvement driven by data that they collect and analyze, schools and leaders should first conduct a needs assessment for their school to identify where to focus improvement efforts. Once they have identified needs, they should set specific improvement goals. Then they should reflect on their teaching and leading practices for further informing improvement. This enables implementing improvement strategies. Another necessary step is to assess progress during and following implementation.

19. B: A school leader can best control the quality of the teaching faculty by developing strategies that address strategic hiring, development, and retention of effective teachers. Hiring effective teachers is important, therefore due diligence must be made to screen candidates and ensure that they have the appropriate skills needed for the classroom and are compatible with school culture. The school leader must provide the appropriate training and development for teachers so that all can grow professionally. Lastly, the school leader must be intentional about retaining effective teachers to reduce the need for hiring.

20. C: Each of the options represents a supportive way of promoting professional development, but choice C is primarily an individual activity and not a way of building up a collaborative learning environment among professionals. Action research is the process of doing informal studies in the school environment to try to find improved practices. While the research is often done alone, the intent of action research is to share with other members of the learning community, making it a collaborative effort in most cases. Professional learning communities (PLCs) are teams of educators who work together to identify concerns and meet needs together and is an excellent way for teachers to improve their skills through professional collaboration. Structured observations are usually something the school administration takes on to ensure a quality control on teaching, but even though it often is top-down oriented, the process is inherently collaborative in that one professional comes and observes another teacher and provides specific feedback to help improve professional practices.

21. B: The new principal is aware that the teachers on campus are not happy; therefore, it is best to talk to a small group of teachers to understand what issues that they have. Sending a survey out is a good strategy, but not necessarily a first step as the data collected may not thoroughly describe the issues that the teachers have, especially if teachers do not feel that they can be honest on the survey. Also, an all-staff meeting can quickly get out of control if outspoken staff persons have unaddressed issues. Sending an email is impersonal and not an advisable first step.

22. B: The action that would best address the challenges in communication, parental engagement, and at home learning is to help the parents learn English by offering ESL classes on campus. Hosting the classes on campus encourages parents to engage with the school community and reinforces that the school values the presence and engagement of the parents. Having a translator on campus and translating documents for parents are important actions to take but are not long-term solutions to the challenge. Students should not be asked to translate school information for their parents.

23. C: All of these questions are important to consider when developing school goals. However, aligning the school goals to the school vision is most critical. The school vision describes how the school is envisioned to be in the future and the school goals are the steps that will enable the school to accomplish that vision.

24. A: State funding under Title I and Smart Start legislation is often available as a way for school leaders to hire school parent facilitators, whose jobs are to involve families in their children's educations. School leaders should not always expect for parents to visit the school. Instead, school leaders should also be visible in the community to facilitate family involvement. School leaders can develop community relationships by beginning with parents who are already involved, but make an effort to involve parents who have not been previously involved. Fostering parental involvement requires two-way communication, not just one-way communication such as robocalls or newsletters.

25. A: According to the US Department of Education's Privacy Technical Assistance Center (PTAC) and the National Institute of Standards and Technology (NIST), a school data breach response *policy* defines staff roles and responsibilities; metrics and standards; and reporting, remediation, and feedback mechanisms. Identifying necessary management support and school resources is a function of the data breach response *plan*. Standardizing response tasks and behaviors and preventing errors from being introduced are functions of *procedures* developed based on the plan. Regular risk assessments are a function not of these components but a recommended broader information management strategy.

26. D: School system guidelines recommend that, in giving teachers observational feedback, school leaders should focus feedback discussions by developing open-ended questions that target specific areas for each teacher, explicitly name two or three teacher strengths they observed, identify one area for improvement that will make the most impact on student learning and teacher development, and develop a few specific and attainable next steps for each teacher to take. Effective observational feedback should include strengths and weaknesses and recommendations for next steps should be clear and attainable.

27. B: Ways that school leaders have appropriately involved students in school improvement efforts include allowing students to plan school-wide forums (A), conduct school-wide surveys (B), participate in hiring school leaders (C), and testify before education committees in their state legislatures, which is legal (D).

28. C: Transparent decision-making is the act of making sure that the process, logic, and rationale used to make a decision are clear and available to be communicated to others. When decision-making is transparent, any critical information used to inform that decision is also readily available to others for review. This transparency allows others to understand how the decision was made.

29. B: All students are expected to meet the standards outlined by the state and federal government. School leaders are responsible for providing students with the instruction, resources, and support necessary to meet these standards. Equity refers to providing students with the resources and support that meet their individual needs. When leaders implement equity in schools, this may mean that some students receive more resources and support or different resources and support than others. This need may be due to a lack of educational opportunity, physical or intellectual disabilities, or other circumstances. Leaders must be aware of what students need so that the right resources and support can be used to support these students. All students will need resources and support to enrich their education, but practicing equity means that students will receive the appropriate amount of resources based on their identified needs.

30. D: Leaders can encourage self-direction in improving among faculty and staff by modeling this behavior. Leaders who are transparent about their own areas of improvement will encourage and set an example for employees. Additionally, the school leader should actively engage employees in self-assessment as well as make resources available for doing so. However, a leader should not leave self-improvement up to employees as it will likely not be done. Employees need support, resources, and encouragement to engage in self-directed improvement.

31. C: Prior to the integration of technology into instructional practice, it was difficult for teachers to individualize instruction for students as it relates to content and pace. Technology applications allow teachers to facilitate instruction that meets the students' individual needs and allows students to work at their own pace toward mastery. Heterogenous student grouping can be a beneficial strategy but is not directly related to technology use in the classroom. Similarly, passive and active learning can occur with or without technology integration. Project-based learning can be facilitated with technology, but it is not a requirement.

32. C: School leaders and others should analyze school data based upon formative classroom assessments and standardized state summative assessments. The data analyzed should include data across grade levels, across school years, by subjects, by student cohorts, by student special populations, and by individual teachers, when possible. Analysis of data should be holistic in order to identify school strengths, needs for improvement, and trends to properly inform the school vision and mission.

33. C: This scenario best represents a mutually beneficial relationship. The church has the benefit of having a meeting place and the principal has the benefit of communicating directly with community members on a regular basis. The other activities help to build positive relationships between the school and the community, but are one-sided.

34. B: School leaders can promote equitable access to curriculum for all students and parents by making staff more comfortable discussing diversity issues, social justice, and values, which will promote equity; clarifying staff misconceptions related to deficit theories about minorities and diverse groups; modeling equity beliefs and behaviors in daily interactions; confronting discrimination and stereotyping in actions and language; creating safe school environments where all students feel welcomed and valued; and establishing support networks for students harassed over cultural, sexual, and/or gender identity.

35. D: In SPBS programs, tier 3 is for the small proportion of students not responding to tier 1 or tier 2 interventions. It involves intensive, individualized interventions tailored to each student. Small socio-emotional group instruction in social and emotional skills, daily student check-in and check-out procedures, and enlisting family support for small-group intervention and instruction are all techniques associated with tier 2.

36. A: Researchers have documented practices of successful school principals relative to developing and sustaining clear school visions and learning goals, including protecting instructional time by scheduling building maintenance and limiting public announcements to minimize disruptions (A); expecting teachers and students to meet the goals they set (B); not only having a clear vision but, when needed, having two visions: one for their school and their own school role and another for their school's change process (C); and ensuring continual progress monitoring related directly to school goals (D).

37. C: To address weak areas, it is better to implement strategies that are backed by research and have been proven to yield good results. This can save the campus the time, effort, and resources that would be wasted if untested and unproven strategies were implemented unsuccessfully. When a leader is looking for strategies to foster change on campus, using research-based and proven best practices is beneficial because there will be a clear direction as to how to successfully implement the strategy and a realistic idea of what results to expect. When untested strategies are implemented, the outcome is less certain. Untested strategies also often take more research and a process of trial and error, or a learning curve, to implement, both of which can delay the implementation of change.

38. C: The goal of professional development is to foster continuous improvement of teaching and learning. Professional development has limited applicability if it is all conducted at the beginning of the school year or at the end of the school year. The best action that the principal can take is to monitor professional development at regular intervals throughout the school year and to encourage teachers to take advantage of timely professional development that can impact their practice during the school year.

39. B: FERPA stands for the Family Educational Rights and Privacy Act. It is a federal law that protects student information and education records.

40. C: Providing ongoing feedback to teachers has the most significant impact on teacher performance. School leaders are responsible for evaluating teachers, providing feedback on evaluations, and assisting teachers with improving areas of weakness through coaching, mentoring, professional development, and other strategies.

41. D: Students must have rigorous instruction in the classroom to be prepared for challenging curriculum in the future. Students who perform well in class but perform poorly on standardized assessments are evidence of misalignment of course work to standardized assessments or inadequate levels of rigor in the classroom. Evaluating the grades of one grade level of students in a specific class is not evidence of ensuring all students are prepared for a challenging curriculum. Reviewing one assessment that was administered prior to enrollment in the school does not demonstrate ongoing monitoring.

42. B: Instruction can be differentiated based on content, process, or product. Differentiating instruction based on product means that the teacher provides multiple ways for a student to demonstrate mastery. Allowing students to write an essay gives students an opportunity to demonstrate mastery in written form or in spoken form. Providing students with different versions of assessments is still assessing students using a test and does not constitute differentiated instruction.

43. A: School leaders should not ask students to serve as translators for their parents who do not speak English. Students may be unreliable translators and should not carry the responsibility of translating, especially in matters that the student may not need to be involved in. For parents who have missed school parent workshops, school leaders can record workshops for parents to watch later. They can create inclusive, welcoming, affirming climates by validating, honoring, and thanking family and community members for supporting the school as well as encouraging and maintaining their meaningful involvement. They can assign parent liaisons, which enable parents to access resources and services that the school offers to families.

44. D: A school leader cannot use their professional influence or position to solicit votes for a candidate on campus. Public school educators have a right to engage in the political process outside of school, but these activities cannot interfere with their job duties or cause a conflict of interest.

45. D: Professional development sessions that take place over time, in contrast to single-session trainings, are more likely to have an impact on teacher performance. Additionally, when a cohort of teachers participates in a training, there is opportunity for collaboration and collective accountability. There are benefits of providing individualized professional development opportunities for teachers. However, when these self-paced trainings are not time bound or accompanied by accountability measures, they are less likely to have a direct impact on current teacher performance.

46. A: A school leader must create structures in the school programming that promote collaboration for teachers. Allotting time in the master schedule for co-planning ensures that teachers will have dedicated time to collaborate, such as by participating in professional learning communities. Offering to pay teachers to stay after school may not be effective because some teachers may opt-out. Additionally, these planning sessions could interfere with other school activities these teachers may be involved in, such as coaching or tutoring. Providing asynchronous collaboration online could potentially be helpful, but it is not the best choice since it likely will not lead to real-time collaboration. Removing qualified teachers for planning can negatively impact student performance and should be used sparingly, if at all.

47. B: Establishing an anti-discrimination policy helps all staff and students to understand the regulations relating to bias and discrimination on campus. Describing what constitutes bias and discrimination makes it easier to identify violations on campus. Additionally, establishing a committee that is focused on cultural awareness and inclusion can help to decrease educational and institutional bias and discriminatory practices. Establishing and enforcing rules has limited efficacy if there is limited understanding of the rationale behind the rules. Having a culturally diverse staff is beneficial, but persons of underrepresented cultures should not be required to teach others about their cultures if they do not choose to. It is beneficial to include opportunities for students to learn about other cultures in the classroom, however this strategy does not help to identify bias and discriminatory practices on campus.

48. B: The majority of female staffs' perception of the supervisor's nicknames as inoffensive could indicate he does not consciously intend disrespect by using them and also suggests a positive relationship between staff and principal. Therefore, reprimanding the supervisor and asking for a public apology is not most appropriate. However, her complaint must be acknowledged and not discredited simply for lack of agreement. As the supervisor's address may not constitute sexual harassment and most staff members do not perceive it as such, a meeting to review laws is also not the best action. The principal should make the supervisor aware of how his habit is perceived by some and that he needs to cease referring to female employees in this manner. School leaders must also defer to policies and procedures outlined by their school board and district regarding sexual harassment, including policies on documentation and reporting.

49. D: New policies should be well communicated in vision and in methodology, but if the policy comes directly from the leadership without having shared motivation the community as a whole will not have buy in and the implementation is likely to face resistance. Delegating authority to staff is a great way of involving stakeholders within the school building but does not include members of the school community who are not employed at the school. Communicating frequently is effective for sharing the vision but does not necessarily motivate community members to participate in implementing new ideas, policies, and procedures.

50. D: Teachers need opportunities to share their beliefs and ideas about teaching and learning with the school leader and with one another. Teachers must believe that they operate in an environment that allows them to be open and honest when examining their own beliefs and practices. Suggestion boxes and surveys are one-way communication tools that do not allow for peer discussion, although anonymity may help teachers feel comfortable giving honest feedback. Providing collaborative meeting time for teachers and meeting with them regularly gives teachers the opportunity to discuss their ideas with one another but also gives them the opportunity to share their ideas with the school leader when they are comfortable.

51. C: Adults learn in more productive ways when the choice to learn is voluntary, when they have choices among learning materials, when they are involved in planning the instruction they will be accessing, and when they are able to give instructors input about how their learning will be assessed.

52. B: When teachers are given the power to choose their own professional development opportunities, they are given the opportunity to reflect on their own practice, identify their strengths and weaknesses, and participate in professional development that they believe is relevant. This contributes to building a risk-taking environment because teachers will be able to examine their own beliefs, values, and practices concerning teaching and learning and determine where they would like to improve.

53. C: Depending on school budget and resources, student needs that are not directly related to student safety and academic performance may not be able to be addressed using school resources. Many community resources used to support schools are targeted toward students in need. These types of resources may address physical needs of students and their families, such as providing food, clothing, toiletries, haircuts and grooming, or helping adults find jobs.

54. B: The principal should consider the campus vision and goals when determining how to allocate resources, including technology resources. The first step that a principal should take when considering spending school funds is determining how the purchase will support the achievement of the vision and goals. When considering upgrading or replacing technology, it is appropriate for the principal to evaluate the current condition of the technology or seek ways to save money; however, the first step that should be taken is to determine if the spending is in alignment with the school goals and vision.

55. B: To provide teachers with effective feedback and collaboration, school leaders must know that student motivation and learning are influenced by different types of assessments; that despite "objective" tests, machine scoring, etc., ultimately assessment is based in the judgment, assumptions, and values of professional educators who design, score, interpret, and grade assessments; that not only is error inevitable in all assessment, but moreover it is typically underestimated; and that reliability in assessment involves scores and results, *not* tests or instruments.

56. A: All the information sources are valid and useful, but a school leader must ensure that the vison and goals of the school align with school, local, state, and federal policies first. After that alignment is confirmed, other information sources can be considered to develop the school's vision and goals.

57. D: While school leaders promote a college-bound culture, they also know that students should be prepared for the career of their choice, which may require specialized training or preparation other than traditional college. In this scenario, the school leader should analyze employment data for the community that the school serves and determine if trends in the data justify adding or changing school programming to meet the needs of the community.

58. D: To mobilize and develop community school support, school leaders should consider that businesses and community-based organizations use different language than educators, and should learn and speak their languages accordingly. School leaders must not only exchange their visions, missions, wants, and needs with those of prospective community partners and identify where these match, they must moreover identify where they overlap, i.e., shared commonalities despite differences. School leaders must show prospective partners how collaboration benefits them. Potential partners have motivations as varied as the community organizations interested in collaborating with schools.

59. C: To partner productively with community members for the shared goal of improving student learning and achievement, schools should take the initiative in offering them information (including school and student data) rather than furnish it only upon request, clearly explain to stakeholders how *all* community members can participate meaningfully, align all collaborative activities directly with the school's vision and goals, and share pertinent, accurate, clear achievement data transparently rather than limiting what they disclose.

60. A: The school leader should make time to collect and analyze student work samples. The audit can be random or the school leader can focus on particular groups of students based on data. However, the school leader should discuss the work samples with the teachers who assigned them. Monitoring grades does not provide the school leader with information about the assignments that were graded. Hosting a science fair and using portfolios for assessment can be beneficial but do not directly indicate that the school leader is involved in these activities.

61. B: Professional Learning Committees (PLC) are designed to facilitate collaboration among teachers based on grade levels, subject area, or other commonalities. In PLCs, educators use quantitative and qualitative data to make decisions about students and are guided by the following questions: What do we want students to learn? What do we do if they do not learn it? What do we do if they learn it? Communicating with parents and submitting reports often include sharing of data, but do not necessarily indicate that the data is used to make decisions. Requiring teachers to host tutorial sessions for students is a beneficial intervention, but may not be a directive based on data.

62. D: The question tests the school leader's understanding of goals directly related to a culture of learning in contrast with other aspects of school performance. Participation in and completion of advanced placement courses is directly related to student learning and reflects high expectations for student academic performance.

63. B: Schools and school leaders use data they have collected for setting goals aligned with their school vision and mission. Data-based decision-making is a best practice for school leaders. Data should be collected for all decision making and data can be collected in the forms of quantitative data, such as standardized assessment results, attendance rates, etc., or qualitative data such as survey feedback. School goals must be aligned with the school vision and mission so that progress toward established goals is connected to achieving the school vision and mission.

64. B: Reading and writing skills are best taught and reinforced within the context of subject matter content. Creating a cross-curricular focus on reading and writing skills would best address the gap in performance among students who are not reading at grade level. Increasing opportunities for students to read is beneficial, but is less effective in closing opportunity gaps, especially when opportunities to engage in reading are voluntary such as after school or at home. Targeted test preparation has limited efficacy if attendance is voluntary and student performance is not monitored.

65. C: All levels, from individual schools to state education departments, must ultimately align with federal policy to make major educational goals match the national vision. However, within this hierarchy, specific expressions of policy, e.g., standardized test instruments, reflect the next higher level. Thus, state standardized tests reflect federal standards, not just state standards; individual schools *directly* apply standards from their school systems, not state standards, which in turn reflect the standards of their school districts, which in turn *directly* apply state standards, not federal standards.

66. A: Traditionally, bus drivers are considered school support staff, typically under the district Transportation Department. They serve multiple school locations and are usually supervised by an employee in the Transportation Department. Custodians and cafeteria workers are often dedicated to one campus and may be supervised by the campus principal. Volunteers are unpaid and not officially school district employees, but are supervised by the campus principal to ensure compliance with policies and procedures. However, school districts may have differing organizational polices and supervision of campus personnel.

67. B: The dean should ask teachers what resources they would like and purchase as many of their suggestions as possible for all teachers. This would increase the number of resources available to teachers and offer them a variety of resources to choose from. Requiring teachers to purchase materials on their own is a disincentive if teachers cannot afford the upfront cost. Professional development is not a resource, it is training. Seeking free or discounted materials does not guarantee that the number and variety of resources will increase on campus if there are limited to no resources available in the local area.

68. B: Community resources can be used in a variety of ways, such as providing school supplies for students, facilitating field trips, and providing mentorship. However, providing tutorial services to students most directly supports student learning. Tutoring students directly impacts student academic performance in class, whereas the other community resources support students' economic and psychosocial needs that may only impact learning indirectly.

69. A: In many American communities and states, schools provide the chief—and often the only—mental health (MH) services that children receive. Parents are more comfortable with such services when they are provided in familiar school settings by familiar staff, rather than avoiding them. Research studies find students are *more* likely to seek counseling services in schools than to look elsewhere. Another reason for school-community collaboration is the necessity of coordinating school and community MH services, not separating them.

70. C: The school budget should be in alignment with the school vision and goals. When facing a budget shortfall, a school leader must scrutinize the budget to determine which areas of spending will most directly impact the school goals. Areas that do not directly impact school goals can have reduced budget allocations or be eliminated entirely.

71. D: According to the National Center for Education Statistics (NCES), school leaders should *not* ignore the political environment because political support and connections can greatly benefit obtaining funding and legislation. They should avoid overly technical language with most stakeholder audiences who will not understand industry jargon. Leaders should communicate with stakeholders in sensitive situations. However, leaders should avoid engaging in large-scale open forums which can obstruct progress by being unfocused, unstructured, and may admit too many voices.

72. C: Student growth is the best data point to inform the principal as to whether the math intervention program was effective and should continue to be funded. Student growth can be calculated by comparing student performance in math at the beginning of the school year to the end of the school year. Although standardized test performance is an important data point, this data alone will not indicate the efficacy of the program, especially for students who may have grown significantly, but not enough to meet standardized test performance requirements.

73. B: A memorandum of understanding is a contract that is used between two parties to outline the details of an agreement in which no money is exchanged. It is an agreement of services to be provided. The verbiage of the memorandum of understanding can be the same as that which is used in a traditional contract. However, the language is often simpler because the sole purpose of the document is to state the exchange of services with no monetary compensation. The purpose of the memorandum of understanding is to document the services to be provided. This type of documentation can be helpful for both parties in providing evidence that the services were agreed upon and delivered.

74. D: To collaborate effectively with teachers regarding assessment, school leaders must know classroom assessment principles, including that no assessment instrument is error free (A)—that is, all assessment involves some error; that authors and users of assessments typically underestimate testing error (B); that reliability, that is, getting consistent results across repeated administrations, applies to test scores and not the tests themselves (C); and that good assessment is not only valid (tests what it means or claims to test) and reliable but also ethical and fair (D).

75. C: The best action that the principal can take to increase the frequency of classroom observations is to plan the observations into the schedule each week. This will force all other appointments and meetings to be scheduled around the classroom observations. Classroom visits should not be left to chance or they will likely not be conducted due to the many tasks that a principal may have to address throughout the day. Additionally, the principal should aim to visit classrooms on different days of the week and times of the day to obtain a well-rounded perspective of teaching and learning on campus.

76. A: No Child Left Behind's stress on accountability has shifted school counselors' responsibilities away from mental health (MH) toward academic performance, reducing professional support services and resulting in limited resources. Students are routinely diagnosed with serious disorders and prescribed costly treatments, despite the fact that prevention and MH promotion can address most issues (B), is representative of inadequate research. The claim that MH resources are not proportionate or equitable (C) represents uneven resource distribution. That cultural traditions marginalize school MH priority (D) represents stigmatizing MH issues.

77. C: Diverse students are frequently overrepresented in special education due to inadequate educator knowledge and/or preparation for distinguishing such differences vs. true disabilities affecting learning and performance. School leaders address this inequity best by analyzing assessment instruments used to evaluate students for special education—which often require accommodations, modifications, or replacement with alternative assessments for diverse learners—rather than grade-level placement procedures because these students need instruction enabling them to perform at grade level, special education teaching strategies, or special curriculum and expectations, all of which are after the fact.

78. D: Based on the research literature, experts draw these conclusions about school principals' roles in creating and realizing school visions and goals, including aligning instruction with them: Principals who focus on school improvement have more effective schools (A). Principals of high-achieving schools have equal confidence in themselves, their schools, and their teachers to meet school goals (B). To be effective, schools need principals who ensure instructional quality rather than delegating this role to others (C). Principals of high-achieving schools communicate to all stakeholders that the most important mission of the school is learning (D).

79. D: The American Psychological Association (APA) recommends a tiered model of behavior management above all others for schools—i.e., a system of positive behavior supports that includes both prevention and intervention with primary, secondary, and tertiary levels—not only for school-wide systems or only for disruptive behaviors of individual students, but for both of these as well as for classroom behavior management.

80. D: The most appropriate response that the principal can offer the PTO president is that the science curriculum purchase directly supports a school goal. All school resources such as curriculum should be aligned to the school vision and goals. Satisfactory student performance is not an appropriate response given that the school leader may have identified college preparation as an area of improvement, even if students were already meeting expectations in this area. Additionally, the cost of the curriculum is irrelevant if the curriculum is not aligned to the campus vision and goals.

81. A: A conflict of interest is a situation in which the school leader can obtain personal gain or harm from a decision they make as school leader. If it is determined that hiring the contractor who is related to the principal would bring the principal personal gain, then the situation could be deemed a conflict of interest.

82. B: School leaders are responsible for ensuring that school safety policies comply with federal, state, and local safety regulations for school physical plants and for communicating all school safety policies to employees, students, and families. They are also responsible for notifying staff and parents in advance of physical plant projects and any other changes that could affect student and staff safety and health. Their responsibilities include developing and revising safety policies with a school health and safety team and other school staff, students, and families, as well as warning parents of painting, pesticides, and other environmental hazards.

83. D: Studies find that, regardless of culture, ethnicity, income, or race, diverse families overall tend to have very similar high aspirations and expectations for their children, care about their success similarly, and (within their means) share similar active involvement in their children's educations.

84. B: The school leader should initially ensure that district resources allocated for the school ELL program are sufficient to meet federal and state program requirements. Basing calculations on the previous fiscal year will not account for changes in the coming year. Basing ELL program resources on the remainder left after allocating the rest to maintain current funding for other programs will not necessarily or likely ensure sufficient funds to meet legal mandates for the ELL program. Evaluating program effectiveness is a later step during and following program administration.

85. A: The logistics function of the ICS identifies services and resources for supporting incident response needs. The planning function collects and evaluates information, identifies incident response issues, develops action plans, and recommends future actions. The command function manages incidents overall and is directly responsible for public safety, information, and community response agency liaisons. The operations function develops objectives, organizes resources, and directs actions and resources for incident responses.

86. D: To help students prepare for their futures, high schools should design curricula relevant to students' lives, communities, and cultural milieus. This includes the career and technical education they will need for today's world, which public high schools must offer. School partnerships with colleges and universities best prepare students for higher education, while community-based and project-based learning best prepare students for employment.

87. A: In a culture of high expectations, staff and students strive towards high goals and excellence. A leader can create a culture of high expectations by setting campus goals above minimum standards. For example, if the expectation is that a school has at least a 90% attendance rate, the leader may set a goal of 95% for the school's attendance rate. Expecting students and staff to perform above minimum expectations creates a culture of high expectations.

88. A: According to the National Education Association (NEA), a school acceptable use policy (AUP) should include a preamble explaining need for an AUP; its goals and development; a school conduct code inclusion of online activity; a definition section of important terms; a policy statement of computer services covered and conditions required for student use (e.g., taking a computer responsibility class); an acceptable uses section *and* unacceptable uses section; and a violations and sanctions section, which should tell students how to report policy violations or question policy application (which may conform to the school disciplinary code), not just define violations.

89. A: Tiered positive behavior support models have been found highly effective as school-wide classroom management systems because they incorporate not only prevention of behavior problems before they occur, but also interventions for existing or developing behavior problems.

Also, by reducing the incidence of problem behaviors, these models provide *more* time for students to be engaged academically.

90. A: A school must hold a Manifestation Determination Review within 10 school days according to the following criteria: if the school is seeking to change student placement for more than 10 consecutive days for disciplinary reasons; if the school suspends a student for disciplinary reasons for more than 10 cumulative days that form a pattern; the school is deciding to expel or otherwise exclude a student for disciplinary reasons; or the school convenes this meeting after a disciplinary incident.

91. B: School districts and state laws may provide guidelines for how school facilities can be utilized by the community. These regulations normally dictate the timeline for requests, any fees that should be assessed, and the types of activities that can occur on school property.

92. D: When school visions are developed through collaboration among employees, they tend to be more appropriate to the contexts of their local school districts, which is an advantage. Collaboratively developed school visions typically are *not* implemented as quickly as those personally developed by school leaders, which also tend to be clearer and more coherent than those developed collaboratively. Collaboratively developed school visions do take longer to develop, slowing change, which is a disadvantage, not an advantage.

93. A: Budget planning and operations coordination are two aspects of using technology to support effective school organization management. Notifying stakeholders of meetings is an aspect of using technology to facilitate effective and timely communication. Collecting, disaggregating, and analyzing different school data is an aspect of using technology to manage information. Facilitating multiple stakeholder contributions to projects is an aspect of using technology to enhance collaboration.

94. D: The first step that a principal must take is to determine the causes of the low morale. Implementing solutions without understanding the causes may lead to wasted time and resources if the solutions do not address the perceived problems. The principal should collect data to identify the issues that staff may have on campus and then develop appropriate solutions.

95. C: It is beneficial to students and the community to build mutually beneficial relationships with various organizations in the community, including medical clinics. The school leader is responsible for ensuring there is documentation such as a memorandum of understanding, logs, or other forms of recordkeeping to document the nature of these relationships and to whom services are provided. The school leader should ensure that there is equitable access to these resources as determined by law, school policy, and the nature of the services provided.

96. C: An integrated management system unites all digital management systems into one total structure, facilitating shared objectives and working as a unit to achieve them. According to experts, a school not using any digital management system is not the best candidate without experience or systems to integrate. A school using one system and not planning more does not need integration. The ideal school uses one or more systems and plans adding more. Systems within an integrated management system share policies, documentation, processes, and procedures; a school wanting these separated does not want integration.

97. D: School leaders must maintain rigorous standards-based instruction across the campus. If students are not able to meet the standards, additional supports and interventions must be offered to students to address educational gaps. The math teacher cannot choose to lower the expectations or standards for students without permission and documentation according to local and state policies. The teacher does not demonstrate a need for training related to implementation of the curriculum, but the teacher must be directed to abide by the curriculum as written.

98. C: Buy in from internal and external community members would be the most likely strategy for engaging stakeholders in the implementation of the school vision and goals. Buy in is achieved when stakeholders are included in the process of developing the school vision and goals. When stakeholders are part of the process, they are more likely to feel ownership of the product which motivates them to engage in implementation. Communicating the school vision and goals to the community is important, but it may not lead to engagement in implementation if stakeholders do not feel that they were including in the process of developing the vision and goals.

99. A: The Supportive School Discipline Initiative (SSDI) included guidance for positive school discipline practices to keep students in school by providing alternatives to exclusionary methods like suspension and expulsion. This guidance was produced jointly by the US Departments of Education and Justice to ensure enforcement of federal civil rights protections against discrimination. It provides school resources with helpful information rather than getting it from them. The SSDI's purpose was to keep student discipline from escalating to the police or prison systems, not to continue this trend.

100. B: The NSBA acknowledges that school districts ARE committed to giving students healthy nutrition. However, it also points out that many school districts, already underfunded, cannot afford the additional expense of meeting the law's stricter nutrition standards as written—particularly because many of its regulations are not funded. Students are going hungry not because the regulations limit food amounts, but because they dislike the food, do not eat it, and so it goes wasted.

101. B: Given that students were consistently performing well in math with the exception of three specific math objectives indicates that there is an issue with the curriculum being used to teach those objectives. Factors such as teacher quality or biased assessments would negatively impact student performance in all objectives, not just a select few and performance would vary from student to student. The most likely reason for students consistently underperforming in the same area despite being taught by different teachers is a misalignment of curriculum to the assessment of the objectives.

102. C: Analyzing videos of one's instructional practices is used in self-assessment and can also support reflection. Rather than relying on the observation feedback of a third party, the teacher can self-assess their proficiency in instructional delivery. Writing in a journal is used in reflection, not for self-assessment.

103. D: The ultimate responsibility of developing and implementing professional development for teachers and staff belongs to the school leader. However, a school leader should leverage the knowledge and expertise of the administrative team and teacher leaders in this process. The school leader may provide the overall vision and goals and delegate some of the responsibilities relating to professional development to others while holding all parties accountable for meeting goals and aligning to the vision.

104. C: School leaders should lead teachers to encourage solid student comprehension of concepts first, and only encourage students to use technology for enhancing their research and problem-solving skills after, not before (A), they understand concepts. They should not only lead but require teachers to instruct students in legal and ethical issues with accessing and using technology (B) and clearly differentiate with teachers between learning targets for student technology skills and learning targets for student thinking and content quality (D).

105. A: Supporting teachers in conducting action research on campus is an example of giving them opportunities to take risks for improving teaching and learning. Action research allows the teacher to identify the area of improvement and hypothesize which actions or strategies may lead to improving the identified area. Action research allows teachers to problem solve using solutions that they have developed which gives them the opportunity to take risks.

106. B: Empirical research into effective practices improving schools and student achievement finds that school leaders overcame resistance to change through proactive strategies, including owning and demonstrating continuing commitment, establishing supportive administrative networks, establishing priorities for change, and communicating with others more intentionally.

107. D: The term decentralization refers to the transfer of power and authority from the school districts to principals to make decisions related to budgets and staffing. In centralized school districts, the central office determines campus spending and the principal has little to no control over how funds are used. In decentralized school districts, principals have greater control over how to use the funds allotted to their school campus.

108. D: School leaders are responsible for knowing and enforcing student and parent rights to privacy and confidentiality of educational records under the Family Educational Rights and Privacy Act (FERPA) and Individuals with Disabilities Education Act (IDEA). They must know and understand exceptions to these laws, which can require them to disclose student records to law enforcement and others. School leaders are responsible for both disclosing information to third parties and obtaining the written parental consent required for such disclosures. They are also responsible for creating policy governing access to student records by parties other than parents and eligible students.

109. A: Community resources used in the school must align with school programming. As a result, resources that will be used in the classroom must align with the curriculum. While it is important to consider a variety of other factors prior to incorporating community resources into the curriculum, it is imperative that the resources are aligned with the school vision and goals, which include the curriculum.

110. D: School leaders should not assign teachers to write technology standards. Integrating technology does help students meet curriculum standards. School leaders and faculty should require students to master any existing technology standards as cross-curricular and procedural knowledge and skills. Experts advise school leaders and teachers to focus not on learning about technology, but on learning with technology.

111. A: Researchers have found that students' academic self-concepts are *not correlated* with their academic achievement, but *are* correlated with later life successes like employment and earnings. Although socioeconomic status (SES) is related to academic self-concept (as well as achievement and retention), it does *not* correlate as strongly with SES as with students' home educational settings. Although smaller school size is found to benefit student participation as well as principal leadership and teacher distributed leadership, *larger* school size correlates positively with student academic self-concept.

112. B: Multiple research studies find that the most effective school leaders are better at identifying the teachers best and worst at increasing student performance among their existing faculty. However, researchers cannot determine whether the fact that effective school leaders also hire the best experienced teachers is more attributable to better leader ability in choosing teachers or to excellent teachers' attraction to schools with the best existing faculty quality. Researchers do observe that school leaders cannot differentiate quality among average teachers as well as they can differentiate better from poorer teachers due to lesser contrast.

113. B: Researchers found that, among public schools, those with higher performance than others each seemed to have a unique combination of factors contributing to their success. These factors include having a clear and shared focus, having high expectations and standards for students, and high levels of family and community involvement. An effective school leader is a significant factor in high performing schools but is not the only determinant of success. Similarly, alignment of curriculum and instruction and frequent monitoring of teaching and learning are critical success factors but cannot be deemed the most important. Finally, schools need resources for success, but many public schools have demonstrated success with meager funding.

114. C: A transactional leader is defined as a leader who is most concerned about performing under the existing policies, rules, and laws. These leaders emphasize compliance and progress toward current goals, often emphasizing strong organizational rigidity and using punishment and reward-based systems of motivation. Transactional leaders are typically able to keep motivation in short term endeavors, but struggle to be adaptable for systemic change. This type of leader is defined in contrast to transformational leaders, who tend to look for possible changes that can be made to improve an existing system. Too much of either leadership style can lead to negative results, so it is recommended to pursue a balance between improving existing systems and striving to perform well within existing systems.

115. A: Teachers and staff have more buy in when changes are made if they are part of the process. Creating a committee that does not include school leadership demonstrates the leader's willingness to give authority to the staff to promote change and a willingness to accept changes that are not generated by leadership. Suggestion boxes and town hall meetings allow staff to share ideas, but these ideas still must be vetted by the school leader as a gate keeper and may not fully address the school's current culture. Teacher engagement in the Shared Decision-Making Committee is vital for school success but will not likely address a campus-wide perception of top-down leadership.

116. A: Almost all aspects of the school program can be supported with community resources. However, stakeholders cannot participate in confidential matters involving personnel or anything else that may violate FERPA laws. Local community organizations can prove to be valuable in a wide array of areas that benefit the school, its staff, and the students, including connecting students with businesses in the community to participate in internships.

117. C: Principals can help staff cope with changes by listening to and validating their thoughts through understanding common internal dialogues. These include wondering whether they will be able to live with and support the vision and also what is needed (A); whether they believe in their and the school's ability to realize it and also in the vision itself (B); whether they will be able to continue long-practiced traditions and why or why not (C); and what the vision will expect of them, how their life will change, and whether they will be able to maintain continuity in instructional practices (D).

118. D: Although each of these options could negatively impact the math performance goal, the loss of a math teacher directly impacts student learning and performance. Student performance in math is directly related to the quality of instruction that students receive in the classroom, meaning that the absence of a qualified math teacher for any length of time can be impactful. Additionally, the unexpected loss of a teacher can be a difficult obstacle to address in a timely manner. It is likely that losing a math teacher would negatively impact the goal.

119. A: Before engaging any community resource, school leaders must consider whether it is compatible with the school's vision and mission. Some resources may have impact in the long-term rather than immediately and should not be discarded because effects will not be seen immediately. Additionally, as communities develop, new resources may be made available. Not all available resources will have a history of prior implementation but may prove beneficial for student learning. Similarly, as the school builds new partnerships, community resources may become available through new community relationships.

120. B: In most public school districts, typically the District Office of Achievement and Accountability makes preliminary enrollment projections to inform school budgets. They do not do this alone because of the difficulty of projecting. Instead, they submit their projections to school leaders, who revise them as needed. School leaders do not project their schools' enrollment alone. Final enrollment projections are made by district committees representing not only the Finance and Student Support offices, but also district Achievement and Accountability and Operations offices.

Constructed Response

1. Essay question graders commonly look for the following elements in a strong response: strong content knowledge, clear organization, and effective arguments or examples. Language and usage are not usually strictly graded, but can make a big impact on the clarity of your ideas.

Please use the provided rubric to make sure your response meets these common criteria. Try to have a friend or family member grade your response for you or take a break after writing your response and return to grade it with fresh eyes.

Constructed Response Rubric

Domain	Description
Content Knowledge	• The response directly addresses every part of the prompt. • The response demonstrates independent knowledge of the topic. • The response discusses the topic at an appropriate depth.
Organization	• The response introduces the topic, usually with a thesis statement or by restating the prompt. • The response directly addresses the prompt by providing a clear and concise answer or solution. • The answer or solution is supported by logical arguments or evidence. • The response restates the main idea in the conclusion.
Arguments and Examples	• The response provides a reasonable answer to the prompt. • The answer is supported by strong reasoning or evidence. • The response develops ideas logically and connects ideas to one another. • The reasoning and evidence provided act to support a unified main idea.
Language and Usage	• The response demonstrates effective use of grammar and uses varied sentence structure throughout the response. • The response demonstrates correct use of spelling, punctuation, and capitalization. • The response demonstrates strong and varied use of vocabulary relevant to the topic and appropriate for the intended audience.

2. Essay question graders commonly look for the following elements in a strong response: strong content knowledge, clear organization, and effective arguments or examples. Language and usage are not usually strictly graded, but can make a big impact on the clarity of your ideas.

Please use the provided rubric to make sure your response meets these common criteria. Try to have a friend or family member grade your response for you or take a break after writing your response and return to grade it with fresh eyes.

Constructed Response Rubric

Domain	Description
Content Knowledge	• The response directly addresses every part of the prompt. • The response demonstrates independent knowledge of the topic. • The response discusses the topic at an appropriate depth.
Organization	• The response introduces the topic, usually with a thesis statement or by restating the prompt. • The response directly addresses the prompt by providing a clear and concise answer or solution. • The answer or solution is supported by logical arguments or evidence. • The response restates the main idea in the conclusion.
Arguments and Examples	• The response provides a reasonable answer to the prompt. • The answer is supported by strong reasoning or evidence. • The response develops ideas logically and connects ideas to one another. • The reasoning and evidence provided act to support a unified main idea.
Language and Usage	• The response demonstrates effective use of grammar and uses varied sentence structure throughout the response. • The response demonstrates correct use of spelling, punctuation, and capitalization. • The response demonstrates strong and varied use of vocabulary relevant to the topic and appropriate for the intended audience.

3. Essay question graders commonly look for the following elements in a strong response: strong content knowledge, clear organization, and effective arguments or examples. Language and usage are not usually strictly graded, but can make a big impact on the clarity of your ideas.

Please use the provided rubric to make sure your response meets these common criteria. Try to have a friend or family member grade your response for you or take a break after writing your response and return to grade it with fresh eyes.

Constructed Response Rubric

Domain	Description
Content Knowledge	• The response directly addresses every part of the prompt. • The response demonstrates independent knowledge of the topic. • The response discusses the topic at an appropriate depth.
Organization	• The response introduces the topic, usually with a thesis statement or by restating the prompt. • The response directly addresses the prompt by providing a clear and concise answer or solution. • The answer or solution is supported by logical arguments or evidence. • The response restates the main idea in the conclusion.
Arguments and Examples	• The response provides a reasonable answer to the prompt. • The answer is supported by strong reasoning or evidence. • The response develops ideas logically and connects ideas to one another. • The reasoning and evidence provided act to support a unified main idea.
Language and Usage	• The response demonstrates effective use of grammar and uses varied sentence structure throughout the response. • The response demonstrates correct use of spelling, punctuation, and capitalization. • The response demonstrates strong and varied use of vocabulary relevant to the topic and appropriate for the intended audience.

4. Essay question graders commonly look for the following elements in a strong response: strong content knowledge, clear organization, and effective arguments or examples. Language and usage are not usually strictly graded, but can make a big impact on the clarity of your ideas.

Please use the provided rubric to make sure your response meets these common criteria. Try to have a friend or family member grade your response for you or take a break after writing your response and return to grade it with fresh eyes.

Constructed Response Rubric

Domain	Description
Content Knowledge	• The response directly addresses every part of the prompt. • The response demonstrates independent knowledge of the topic. • The response discusses the topic at an appropriate depth.
Organization	• The response introduces the topic, usually with a thesis statement or by restating the prompt. • The response directly addresses the prompt by providing a clear and concise answer or solution. • The answer or solution is supported by logical arguments or evidence. • The response restates the main idea in the conclusion.
Arguments and Examples	• The response provides a reasonable answer to the prompt. • The answer is supported by strong reasoning or evidence. • The response develops ideas logically and connects ideas to one another. • The reasoning and evidence provided act to support a unified main idea.
Language and Usage	• The response demonstrates effective use of grammar and uses varied sentence structure throughout the response. • The response demonstrates correct use of spelling, punctuation, and capitalization. • The response demonstrates strong and varied use of vocabulary relevant to the topic and appropriate for the intended audience.

Practice Test #2

Selected-Response Questions

1. The dean of instruction of a ninth-grade high school academy would like to monitor student progress for the grading period. Which of the following sources of data would best inform the dean of student progress?

a. Student portfolios of work samples from previous and current marking periods
b. Benchmark scores from the previous and current marking periods
c. Anecdotal teacher notes
d. Report card grades for the marking period

2. Which statement is accurate about why classroom management systems are effective?

a. By making learning environments orderly, they enable student academic success.
b. They control student behavior rather than helping emotional-social development.
c. They work by increasing prosocial behavior rather than academic engagement.
d. They work by providing individualized intensive interventions for all students.

3. A school leader is new to the community and attends a district school board meeting. In what way can attending this meeting best support the development of this school leader's beliefs about educational issues?

a. By displaying the diverse issues and viewpoints across the unfamiliar school district
b. By demonstrating the areas of disagreement within a school district
c. By allowing the school leader the opportunity to learn how to run school board meetings
d. By shedding light on differences between a school's vision and the district vision

4. Many types of mental health challenges can be caused or exacerbated by environmental stimuli, such as a school environment. These same challenges are also often difficult to effectively address by intervention at the school level. Which of the following types of mental health challenges is LEAST likely to be caused by or addressed within a school context?

a. External stressors
b. Educational problems
c. Psychosocial problems
d. Psychological disorders

5. A middle school is expecting a dramatic increase in the number of students requiring special education services for the upcoming school year. Which of the following should be the principal's primary concern?

a. How this group of students will impact current student performance data
b. The availability of human and fiscal resources needed to meet the needs of this group of students
c. Community resources for this group of students
d. The reason for the increase in the number of students requiring special education

6. Which of the following best describes shared leadership?

a. Authoritarian leadership
b. The delegation of authority and responsibility to other team members
c. Consulting others before making decisions
d. Publicly recognizing stakeholders that demonstrate leadership

7. Which of the following actions best exemplifies a focus on school-wide rigorous curriculum and standards-based instruction?

a. Increase the number of advanced placement and dual credit courses offered on the master schedule.
b. Increase the number of students taking college entrance exams.
c. Evaluate campus-based assessments for alignment to the standards and curriculum and revise where appropriate.
d. Offer after-school tutorials for students who are falling behind.

8. Which of the following best illustrates the connection between the school community and local employment trends?

a. A school begins to offer health care courses and training in response to a need for more healthcare workers in the community.
b. The school librarian partners with the neighborhood library to share resources.
c. A school sets a goal to increase the graduation rate.
d. A school increases the number of dual-credit college courses offered on campus.

9. What is the primary benefit of conducting teacher evaluations?

a. Evaluations can provide feedback to staff members so that they can grow professionally.
b. Evaluations are needed to determine who is not performing to expectations.
c. Evaluations can help identify the professional development and coaching that teachers need.
d. Evaluations can be used to remove an underperforming teacher from their position.

10. A student reports to the principal that a teacher helped him with answers on the state standardized test. Which of the following should the principal do next?

a. Investigate to find out if the student is telling the truth.
b. Confront the teacher accused of cheating.
c. Document the complaint in case the school is audited.
d. Report the allegation to the district testing department.

11. Of the following, which correctly reflects characteristics of school professional development that will best meet student needs and achieve school goals?

a. It should be provided exclusively to professional teachers and faculty.
b. It should be separated from the job to enable greater perspective.
c. It should be differentiated to address individual areas of challenge.
d. It should be provided periodically but regularly by being scheduled.

12. The school principal institutes a professional learning community made up of social studies and reading teachers from grades six through eight. This professional learning community is an example of which of the following?

a. Horizontal alignment of curriculum and instruction
b. Vertical alignment of curriculum and instruction
c. Horizontal and vertical alignment of curriculum and instruction
d. Cross-cultural integration of curriculum and instruction

13. A school leader conducts a needs assessment for the school using student academic performance data, student attendance data, student focus groups, and teacher focus groups. The leader then decides to conduct an anonymous survey of community stakeholders. The primary benefit of this action is that:

a. The leader will increase buy in from the community.
b. Surveying the community will increase community engagement.
c. The school leader will be able to explain past school performance.
d. The school leader will have multiple sources of data to conduct a thorough needs assessment.

14. A high school principal determines that it is no longer financially viable to sponsor the fine arts program at the school. Enrollment in fine arts courses has steadily decreased over the past four school years and the expenses of the program have exceeded the budget. However, the principal knows that many stakeholders in the community feel strongly about having a fine arts program. Which of the following represents the best action for the school principal?

a. Continue to offer the fine arts program.
b. Make an announcement to the students and staff that there will not be a fine arts program next year.
c. Host a fundraiser for the fine arts program.
d. Host a meeting to explain to stakeholders the reasons for eliminating the fine arts program.

15. The athletics director received notice that there will be random drug testing of all student athletes next week. The principal discovers that the athletics director acted against policy and advised all of the coaches to inform students of the upcoming drug test. Which of the following actions should the principal take next?

a. Give the athletics director a written reprimand for breaching policy.
b. Document the infraction in the athletics director's personnel file.
c. Inform the athletics department of the information breach.
d. Remove the athletics director from his or her position.

16. Which of the following statements correctly reflects considerations for school leaders in supporting school improvement through effective resource management?

a. The school vision and goals are most dependent upon physical resources.
b. Material resources are priority as they are needed for a safe, comfortable teaching and learning environment.
c. Fiscal resource management is necessary for managing other resources, with some exceptions.
d. Human resource management is necessary for smaller class sizes and optimal student learning and achievement.

17. A school principal would like to develop a positive partnership with the school community. Which of the following actions would best help the principal to achieve this goal?

a. Publish a monthly school newsletter with reminders for important school events.
b. Host a student award ceremony each semester to highlight school and student successes.
c. Attend all school athletic events.
d. Send a survey to all community members to get their feedback on school performance.

Refer to the following for questions 18–20:

The school principal reviews classroom observation and feedback with assistant principals weekly but often has very few classroom observations of their own conducted in preparation for the weekly meeting. This week, a teacher complained to the principal that the feedback from their most recent evaluation was not fair because it did not provide a well-rounded view of their performance.

18. When increasing the frequency of classroom visits, which of the following should NOT be considered when the school principal observes teachers in their classrooms?

a. The quality and rigor of assignments given to students.
b. The implementation of strategies learned in professional development sessions.
c. Classroom environment and culture.
d. The teacher's tenure or contract status.

19. Other than classroom observations, which of the following would best provide an additional source of data for the principal to evaluate the teacher on?

a. Student performance data
b. Student surveys
c. Parent surveys
d. Teacher self-assessments

20. Which of the following is the best action that the principal can take to address this teacher's concern?

a. Conduct additional observations of the teacher at various days of the week, times of the day, and in varied circumstances.
b. Explain why the evaluation was accurate.
c. Find other staff members who can confirm what was written in the teacher's evaluation.
d. Show the teacher that all protocols and policies were followed in conducting the evaluation.

21. A school is in the process of implementing a campus-wide adoption of new technology. Which of the following is LEAST central to the role of a school leader acting to implement this change?

a. Leading by example and using technology with teachers and students
b. Attending professional development classes and keeping current with the research
c. Establishing conditions for change by setting high learning expectations and encouraging teacher effort
d. Encouraging use of the new technology, offering teachers learning opportunities, and resolving implementation problems

22. On which of the following should educators mainly base their education practices?

a. Traditions in educational practice
b. Educators' personal experiences
c. Action research
d. Peer-reviewed research and best practices

23. Which of the following best describes rigorous instruction?

a. Curriculum and instruction that is challenging to students
b. Honors, advanced placement, and dual credit courses
c. Appropriate grading and feedback on student work
d. Teaching above student grade levels

24. At the midway point of the school year, the school leader is surprised to find that the school is not on track to achieve the school goals for the year. What could the school leader have done to prevent being surprised by this information?

a. Established a plan for assessing and monitoring progress at regular intervals.
b. Delegated responsibilities to the leadership team.
c. Communicated the goals more effectively to stakeholders.
d. Created a committee to engage with the leader in the development of the goals.

25. A school leader would like to increase the use of differentiated instruction as an instructional strategy on campus. Which of the following actions would be most effective in achieving this goal?

a. Publicly recognize teachers who use differentiated instruction in the classroom.
b. Purchase books about differentiated instruction and distribute them to all teachers.
c. Model differentiated instruction during professional development sessions and monitor classroom implementation.
d. Hire an instructional coach that can train teachers how to use differentiated instruction in the classroom and evaluate their efficacy.

26. What is most accurate regarding social and emotional learning (SEL) programs that schools often offer in conjunction with school-wide positive behavior support (SPBS) programs?

a. Programming is implemented at individual grade levels
b. Programming requires quarterly monitoring
c. Programming includes practicing opportunities
d. Programming is limited to the school environment

27. A leader must ensure that the school's physical plant, equipment, and support systems operate safely, efficiently, and effectively. Which of the following strategies best helps the school leader fulfill this responsibility?

a. Walking the campus two times a day to check for safety
b. Soliciting feedback about the campus from teachers and staff
c. Selecting the appropriate staff to manage the physical plant
d. Reviewing all inspection reports monthly

28. The federal Supportive School Discipline Initiative (SSDI) issued a (2014) positive school discipline guidance package. Why did the US Department of Justice (DOJ) collaborate with the US Department of Education (ED) in producing this resource?

a. To make school discipline consistent with justice and correctional systems
b. To address inevitable student justice involvement by disciplinary exclusion
c. To ensure that Civil Rights Act titles prohibiting discrimination are enforced
d. To establish disciplinary practices to keep juvenile offenders out of school

29. A school's crisis response plan includes a "command and control" framework identifying personnel responsible for directing crisis response. What must school leaders assure most to make this aspect of the plan as effective as possible?

a. Select longest-term employees with the most familiarity of school operations. .
b. During a crisis, distribute leadership of command and control among several members.
c. Clearly define responsibilities for each identified member in advance for various crises.
d. During a crisis, have each command and control member report to at least two others.

30. Which of the following categories represents the highest percentage of budgetary expenditures for public schools?

a. Student support services
b. Operations
c. Instruction and instruction related
d. Administration

31. Which of the following is the best example of how school leaders can support teachers in developing their expertise and leadership skills?

a. School leaders should increase teachers' workloads to give them opportunity to demonstrate responsibility.
b. School leaders should develop all teachers in the same way to avoid building resentment among staff.
c. School leaders must create safe environments for teachers' risk-taking and creative ideas.
d. School leaders should limit how much authority to share with teachers to prevent diminishing their own authority.

32. Which of the following actions would be most effective for ensuring that shared vision and goals are implemented consistently?

a. Publishing regular updates regarding goal progress in the school newsletter and on the school website
b. Identifying barriers and challenges to vision implementation as quickly as possible and revising plans to address them
c. Delegating responsibility to others to assist with vision implementation, monitoring goal progress regularly, and holding all staff members accountable for fulfilling their roles in the implementation plan
d. Meeting regularly with internal and external stakeholders to solicit feedback and ideas regarding vision and goal implementation

33. A principal has received notice that the current standards will be phased out and a new set of standards will be adopted for the upcoming school year. Which of the following actions should the principal take first regarding curriculum development and revision?

a. Set aside money in the school budget for purchasing new curriculum.
b. Create a committee to advise the principal on curriculum adoption.
c. Plan dates for training teachers about the new curriculum.
d. Identify what standards are changing and how the current curriculum and resources align to the new standards.

34. The first year of a mentoring pilot program has been completed. The first year was free for the school, but the school will have to pay a fee if the mentoring program is to continue for subsequent years. Which of the following would best inform the principal's decision about whether to continue the program?

a. The number of students who participated in the program
b. Student feedback on the program
c. Community feedback on the program
d. Student performance indicators related to the campus goals

35. Which of the following is true about mental health and student learning and achievement?

a. Educational problems are not related to mental health issues.
b. External stressors can create obstacles to learning and achievement.
c. Only psychological disorders diagnosed by a health professional can be addressed in schools.
d. Only students who qualify for special education services can receive support for mental health issues.

36. A school leader is monitoring the curricular programs to determine whether student needs are being met. Which of the following would provide the most valid indication that the curricular programs are meeting student needs?

a. Assessment data shows that students are meeting minimum performance standards.
b. Parent survey data demonstrates that parents are pleased with the curricular programs.
c. Teacher observations are generally positive.
d. Assessment data shows that most students are demonstrating academic growth.

37. Surveyed school principals have reported that which of the following has been adversely affected since standards-based accountability systems were implemented?

a. Teacher morale
b. Curriculum and instruction
c. Student assessment practices
d. Expectations and achievement

38. In school-wide positive behavior support programs, which level typically involves school-wide practices that support positive behaviors for all students?

a. Tier 1
b. Tier 2
c. Tier 3
d. Tier 4

39. Which of the following actions best illustrates how a school leader engages with the community in a proactive manner?

a. The school leader attends all local school board meetings.
b. The school leader attends the community holiday parade.
c. The school leader hosts an award ceremony for students at the school.
d. The school leader purchases advertisement space in the local community newspaper.

40. Which kind of data best helps teachers to identify strengths and needs in their teaching practices, support capacity-building, and identify specific remedial student groups?

a. Formative data
b. Summative data
c. Student profiles
d. Enrollment data

41. Which of the following situations represents an issue of ethics?

a. The football coach obtained a sponsorship from a local restaurant to provide snacks for students during football practice.
b. A group of students make a request to form a club for students who were adopted.
c. The debate sponsor uses money collected from students for fees to pay for his lunch but replaces the money after school.
d. A pastor from a local church donates table linens to the drama department for an upcoming banquet.

42. A school leader is approached by a journalist to contribute to a news segment about preparing students for an upcoming standardized test. Which of the following actions should the school leader take first?

a. Prepare a statement for the news segment.
b. Contact the school district media department.
c. Schedule a date for the interview.
d. Identify students who can also participate in the news segment.

43. A school leader is developing a plan for improving teaching on campus and has identified several effective teachers in the math department. How should the school leader best incorporate these teachers into the plan?

a. Request that the teachers mentor low-performing teachers.
b. Allow the teachers to continue teaching using their current best practices.
c. Recognize the teachers for their effective performance.
d. Allow the teachers to identify areas in which they would like to grow and provide resources and support.

44. A staff member who used to perform their job consistently begins completing tasks after due dates and has started being absent without a reasonable excuse. Which of the following describes a school leader's best course of action to address this staff member?

a. The school leader should give some of the staff member's responsibilities to someone else who is more reliable.
b. The school leader should recommend that the staff member seek mental health and counseling services.
c. The staff member should be terminated.
d. The staff member should be transferred to another department.

45. Which of the following describes a role of parents and other community members as it relates to educator professional development (PD)?

a. Holding educators accountable for results
b. Understanding which student learning needs are presenting difficulties for educators
c. Demanding and supporting quality PD that improves teaching, leadership, and achievement
d. Allotting time and facilitating PD that will help educators address student learning problems

46. For managing school food services, the FDA refers to seven Hazard Analysis and Critical Control Point (HACCP) principles. Which of the following lists these principles in the correct sequence?

a. Identifying CCPs, determining critical limits to control hazards, hazard analysis, planning corrective actions, establishing CCP monitoring procedures, record-keeping system, verification procedures.
b. Hazard analysis, identifying CCPs, determining critical limits to control hazards, establishing CCP monitoring procedures, planning corrective actions, verification procedures, record-keeping system.
c. Verification procedures, determining critical limits to control hazards, identifying CCPs, establishing CCP monitoring procedures, hazard analysis, record-keeping system, planning corrective actions.
d. Determining critical limits to control hazards, identifying CCPs, establishing CCP monitoring procedures, verification procedures, record-keeping system, planning corrective actions, hazard analysis.

47. A parent of a student with a disability informs the principal that they overheard two teachers making fun of their child's disability during dismissal. Which of the following is the most appropriate response that the principal should make to the parent?

a. Inform the parent that they have permission to pick their child up from school early.
b. Inform the parent that the teachers will be disciplined.
c. Assure the parent that the described behavior is not tolerated, and an investigation will occur.
d. Assure the parent that the teachers will no longer have dismissal duty.

48. Several community members have expressed concern to the school principal about the rate of teen suicide and believe that the principal should be proactive in promoting the mental health and wellbeing of students on campus. The school leader believes this is a helpful suggestion. Which of the following would be the best action to take to address the community members' concern?

a. Write an article in the school bulletin about teen suicide.
b. Begin a counseling and wellness program on campus that refers students to community agencies and resources.
c. Hang posters in the school hallways promoting a 24-hour suicide hotline.
d. Ban social media use on campus to prevent cyberbullying.

49. Which of the following factors should a school leader consider first when scheduling a meeting with a large group of parents?

a. The languages that the parents speak
b. The availability of funds to serve refreshments
c. The day of the week and time of the day to host the meeting
d. The school leader's schedule

50. The school principal informs the leadership team that she will participate in a six-week program to improve her leadership skills. This action best illustrates that:

a. The principal is a model for continuous professional growth.
b. The principal has weaknesses that need to be addressed.
c. The principal is self-reflective.
d. The principal is an effective leader.

51. Students of XYZ High School will each receive a laptop for school use at the beginning of the school year. The school dean is tasked with developing an acceptable use policy for students. What is the primary benefit of creating an acceptable use policy for students?

a. To encourage students to take care of the devices
b. To help students learn how to use technology to engage in instruction
c. To teach students how to conduct themselves online
d. To clearly communicate how the device should be used and the consequences for not abiding by the policy

52. Which of the following strategies best addresses the achievement gap?

a. Disaggregating student data by subpopulations to identify disparities in performance
b. Providing targeted interventions to students who perform unsatisfactorily
c. Tracking student performance and making projections about future performance based on past performance
d. Exempting struggling students from meeting certain standards

53. Which of the following statements does not support standardized classroom practices and procedures?

a. Improving the cost-efficiency of school programs by reducing differentiation
b. Increasing the conformity to curricula within departments
c. Promoting safety throughout the school
d. Ensuring that students can expect the same teaching style from each teacher

54. A group of parents expressed concern to the school leader that they did not feel involved in the decision-making processes at the school. Which of the following actions could the school leader take to address their concerns?

a. Place a suggestion box in the front office of the school.
b. Create a parent focus group.
c. Invite parents to register as volunteers at the school.
d. Create an email newsletter to distribute to parents monthly.

55. Which of the following strategies would be most effective for communicating with stakeholders who speak a different language?

a. Hire translators and provide translation machines at community events.
b. Hire a bilingual principal.
c. Translate all written communications.
d. Ask students to translate for their parents.

56. Which of the following is indicative of a school that is focused on encouraging intercultural awareness in students?

a. Social studies classrooms are required to include one research project per year that focuses on different cultures.
b. The principal invites African American guest speakers to the campus for Black History Month.
c. The principal publishes a statement about diversity and inclusion on the school website.
d. The principal adds American Sign Language to the foreign language course offerings.

57. According to research findings, transformational school leaders are most effective in promoting organizational learning. Which of the following best reflects how they do this?

a. By demonstrating their high expectations for students
b. By demonstrating their high expectations for teachers
c. By modeling ongoing learning and providing opportunities for staff to learn from peers
d. By researching effective instructional practices and training staff to implement them

58. Which of the following is the best evidence of clear and effective communication regarding the school vision and goals?

a. Stakeholders who understand the vision and goals can articulate them in their own words.
b. Stakeholders can memorize the school vision and goals.
c. Stakeholders offer suggestions for revision of the school vision and goals.
d. Stakeholders support the school vision and goals.

59. The math department is excited that for the third consecutive time, most of the seventh-grade students have earned perfect scores on their six-week report cards. The dean of instruction is concerned by this news and requests to examine student work samples and class grades. Which of the following is a likely reason that the dean is concerned?

a. The data may indicate that the students are not receiving rigorous curriculum and instruction.
b. The math department may have misinterpreted the student data.
c. The few students who did not receive perfect grades may be falling behind.
d. The students are likely committing acts of academic dishonesty.

60. Which of the following best describes how the school leader should evaluate the technology data systems they use?

a. Does the data system provide the data necessary to support the work of collaborative data teams?
b. Is the technology data system affordable?
c. Is the technology data system user friendly?
d. Do other schools use this technology data system?

61. Which of the following does not demonstrate that an education leader proactively addresses challenges to student emotional safety?

a. The education leader collaborates with the school counselor to design a referral system for students experiencing an emotional or mental crisis.
b. The education leader provides information about free resources in the community for mental health needs to all parents and stakeholders at the beginning of the school year.
c. The education leader creates a grief counseling group following the suicide of a student.
d. The education leader schedules a counselor to visit the school monthly.

62. The dean of students informs the school principal that discipline data shows that a disproportionate number of black students have been suspended from school for the first semester when compared to the general population of students. Which of the following represents the best action that the principal could take?

a. Identify a mentoring program for black students on campus.
b. Assess the school culture to determine if there are negative assumptions or beliefs that impact teaching and learning.
c. Send an email to teachers that no black students can be suspended for the second semester.
d. Identify teachers who should attend classroom management training.

63. A group of teachers who are unhappy with some of the policies on campus have organized into an informal group. They have begun inviting other teachers and staff to meet with them to discuss campus concerns. The school leader has become aware of the group. Which of the following is the best response to the formation of this group?

a. Invite the group to meet with the school leader to discuss their concerns.
b. Create a new campus policy banning the formation of groups without permission.
c. Administer a survey to the staff to gather their opinions about campus policies.
d. Require that the group only meet off campus outside of school hours.

64. A school leader has created a committee of staff members on campus that will serve as an advisory board for accomplishing the school vision. Members include the administrative team, school counselors, teacher leaders, and support staff. The most likely result of this action would be that:

a. The decision-making process will be slowed down because more people are involved.
b. Staff turnover will be reduced.
c. The leader will be viewed as a poor decision-maker.
d. Staff will be supportive of the vision and will help to accomplish their assigned roles.

65. School leaders and teachers are frequently frustrated about lack of family and community school involvement, particularly in diverse populations. Which is the most likely source of difficulty?

a. Educator attitudes are often unrealistic.
b. Educators attempt to use too many methods.
c. Educator efforts are often very intense.
d. Educator engagement is lacking.

66. Which of the following represents an effective step that a school leader can take to change negative assumptions about teaching diverse populations?

a. Conduct diversity training with all staff.
b. Create a mentoring program on campus.
c. Publish an official statement on diversity and inclusion.
d. Only hire teachers that represent the student demographics.

67. Which of the following represents a principle informing school leader support and professional development (PD) of teachers throughout their careers?

a. PD must be continuing and supported by repetition and follow-up to change teaching over time.
b. PD for teachers should be focused on practice and not on theoretical bases.
c. PD is best administered as a stand-alone process within individual schools.
d. When school leaders furnish PD, they should be sure to include the newest, most popular topics.

68. Which of the following best illustrates the connection between the school community and local education trends?

a. A school creates an internship program for students interested in working in the healthcare industry.
b. Recruiters from local colleges set up booths in the school cafeteria during lunch time to inform students about their school choices.
c. Graduates of the local community college mentor high school seniors.
d. A school offers a college math preparation course based on the math skills needed for success at the local community college.

69. What is a result of school leaders' community outreach for partnerships with schools?

a. Community partners are more informed about schools, but do not feel ownership.
b. Community partners who personally help students learn do not expect any thanks because of mutual benefits.
c. Community access to school facilities only benefits the community, not the school.
d. Community members understand schools better by accessing their facilities and events.

70. Which of the following represents the most effective way that a leader can ensure the staff members under their supervision act in an ethical manner?

a. Writing and distributing policies and procedures
b. Actively monitoring employee behavior
c. Requiring employees to sign a form to acknowledge receipt of the staff handbook
d. Responding to reports of unethical behavior immediately

71. The math teachers on campus suggest to the school leader that improved academic performance in math should be one of the school's goals. The school leader agrees and decides to create a measurable goal for student math performance. Which of the following is the best example of a measurable math performance goal?

a. 95% of eighth-grade students will demonstrate growth in their math class.
b. All eighth-grade students will be successful in their math class.
c. Eighth-grade students will earn at least a B average in their math class.
d. 90% of eighth-grade students will earn at least a B average in their math class.

72. A school leader and the leadership team have begun developing a plan for implementing the school goals. The leader has identified the necessary action steps, the persons responsible for each step, and the time frames in which each step should be taken. Which of the following is the most appropriate next step for finalizing the plan?

a. Identify the resources needed for each step and evidence of implementation.
b. Share the plan with persons who will be responsible for completing an action step.
c. Present the plan to staff.
d. Plan future meetings with staff to monitor progress in implementing the plan.

73. School leaders must know of a wide range of mental health professionals available to students. To which of the following are students most often referred for help that schools cannot provide?

a. Career counselors
b. Family counselors
c. Group counselors
d. School counselors

74. The school participates in a health education program that provides sex education and contraceptives to middle school students. A teacher is opposed to this program and becomes very vocal in the community about the dangers of having this program on campus. The principal begins to receive numerous phone calls and emails about the program. Which of the following actions would best help the principal refocus attention to vision and goals?

a. Issue a public statement regarding the value of health education and the alignment of the program with the school's vision.
b. Meet with the teacher who is opposed to the program to reach an agreement.
c. Ignore the phone calls and emails.
d. Hold a community meeting to discuss the program with stakeholders.

75. An elementary school leader has set a goal of establishing a school climate wherein all educators believe every child can learn and succeed, and are committed to enabling every child to do so. Which classroom practice should the leader encourage teachers to use toward this goal?

a. Differentiating instruction
b. Assigning student teams to compete in contests
c. Differentiating assessment standards by student
d. Regularly researching individual student interests

76. All of the following demonstrate that the school leader conducts self-reflection EXCEPT:

a. Reading books and articles related to the field of education and leadership practice
b. Keeping a journal
c. Evaluating one's self using the personnel evaluation rubric
d. Attending a mandated training

77. When selecting professional development for staff, which of the following should a leader consider first?

a. The cost of the professional development
b. Whether the professional development has been effective on other campuses
c. The areas of deficit of staff based on observations and evaluations
d. The alignment of the professional development with the campus vision and goals

78. During a classroom observation, a school leader notices that a student is sitting in the corner of the classroom and is not engaged in the lesson. The teacher does not attempt to engage the student during the lesson. When the school leader meets with the teacher about the observation and asks about the student, the teacher responds that there was no point in trying to get that student to participate because he was going to fail no matter what. The teacher's response demonstrates a disagreement with which educational philosophy?

a. Teach students to be life-long learners.
b. Education is the key to success.
c. All students can learn.
d. Educate the whole child.

79. A school principal reflects on their personal performance during the most recent school year. Based on data and their own reflection, the principal noticed that many of the plans that were created at the beginning of the school year were not implemented properly because he or she was not able to get all of the action items done. Which of the following action plans might help the principal improve time management in the future?

a. Use data to make more effective decisions.
b. Prioritize activities that are most directly related to the campus vision and goals.
c. Hold members of the leadership team accountable for their task completion.
d. Increase the number of hours that he or she spends on campus.

80. Which of the following best describes the relationship between the school principal and the school board?

a. The school principal recommends the hiring and termination of teachers to the school board.
b. The school principal reports campus data to the school board at board meetings.
c. The school board elects or hires and supervises the superintendent, who in turns hires and supervises the school principal.
d. The school board implements state and local policies that the principal must abide by.

81. A middle school principal wants to improve the quality of teaching and learning on campus on a continuous basis throughout the school year rather than only reviewing annual performance data and making changes prior to the start of the school year. Which of the following strategies would best help the principal to achieve this goal?

a. Assess students every six weeks using benchmark exams and use the data to adjust the instructional program.
b. At the start of the school year, administer a comprehensive exam to determine what information students retained over the summer.
c. Administer a comprehensive exam to students at the beginning of the school year, in the middle of the school year, and at the end of the school year and use the data to make plans for the following school year.
d. Require that teachers maintain portfolios for all students to demonstrate learning and growth over the course of the school year.

82. For the third subsequent year, a school leader has had 40 percent turnover of teaching staff. This high rate of turnover has impacted the campus negatively and the school leader wants to address this concern. In a stakeholder meeting, the leader asks members to brainstorm suggestions for addressing teacher retention. Which of the following suggestions should the school leader implement first?

a. Administer a survey to teachers to get their feedback on what they like and dislike about working at the campus.
b. Petition the district to raise teacher salaries.
c. Offer bonuses to teachers who produce good student performance results on standardized assessments.
d. Provide mentors to new teachers on campus.

83. When using student outcome data to monitor school improvement progress, which of these would indicate a need to update the school improvement plan?

a. Data show improvement goals taking longer to be met than planned.
b. Data show that the school is on target to meet expected goals.
c. Data can be monitored more frequently due to acquisition of improved technology applications.
d. Data show that the school lags behind other schools with similar student populations.

84. A middle school principal has been informed that there will be a cut in the school budget in the area of technology capital for the upcoming school year. Based on this information, which of the following represents the best action that the school principal could take?

a. Do not offer a technology class for students for the upcoming school year.
b. Assess the current technology on campus and determine how to use current assets for next school year's instruction.
c. Apply for local grants to compensate for the budget cut.
d. Ask the community for donations of technology equipment.

85. Which of the following is the best evidence of effective monitoring of progress toward the vision and goals?

a. The leader implements clear checkpoints and milestones for goal activities.
b. The leader provides regular updates to stakeholders regarding progress toward the vision and goals.
c. Student performance data shows evidence of growth.
d. An advisory committee meets regularly to provide feedback to the leader regarding the vision and goals.

86. Which of the following would be the most effective way to engage parents in student behavior management systems?

a. Distribute the behavioral code of conduct to parents at the beginning of the school year.
b. Find parent volunteers to help enforce the behavioral code of conduct.
c. Ask for feedback from parents on the draft of the behavioral code of conduct before it is finalized.
d. Develop a behavioral code of conduct in partnership with teachers, parents, and students.

87. The National Association of Secondary School Principals (NASSP) recommends that school leaders furnish comprehensive staff development in supporting student mental health. Which area of recommended training is most related to the Response to Intervention (RtI) model?

a. Early identification of students having or at risk of mental disorders
b. The use of referral mechanisms for school and community services
c. Strategies to apply in promoting school-wide positive environments
d. Models for consultation, coordination, and collaboration in schools

88. To inform professional development methods, which of the following is the best format for adult learners, based on the principles of adult learning?

a. Formal
b. Directive
c. Hands-on
d. Theoretical

89. A school leader is managing a significant structural change on campus. Which of the following strategies would be most effective in managing change?

a. Develop goals related to the new changes.
b. Obtain buy in from stakeholders by allowing them to have input.
c. Provide professional development opportunities that will equip teachers to be successful with the new changes.
d. Replace staff who are not on board with the changes.

90. Which of the following strategies is most effective for communicating school and student success to families and the community?

a. Publishing a monthly school newsletter
b. Sending weekly automated calls
c. Sending letters home with students
d. Hosting monthly community meetings

91. ABC Elementary School receives permission to participate in a television news media segment about keeping children active. The principal would like all of the students in the soccer club to participate in the filming of the news segment. What should the principal do first?

a. Inform the teachers that the media will be on campus.
b. Meet with the students to set expectations for behavior when they are being filmed.
c. Inform the community that the school will be participating in the news segment.
d. Ensure that all students who plan to participate have a media release form signed by a parent on file.

92. A new student arrives from Switzerland, speaks French, and is enrolled in XYZ High School. The only languages spoken at the school are English and Spanish. Which of the following actions should the school leader take in order to accommodate the needs of this student?

a. Research Swiss culture.
b. Pair the student with a peer to help the student get acclimated.
c. Hire a translator to help communicate with the student during classes.
d. Meet with the student and their family to discuss their needs using a temporary translator if possible.

93. What does the National Association of Secondary School Principals (NASSP) recommend regarding effectively using community support outside the school to promote student mental health (MH)?

a. Providing community service personnel in schools' comprehensive staff development is excluded.
b. Providing school staff training in promoting positive school-wide environments is found ineffective.
c. Providing school staff training in how to use mechanisms to refer students to community services is effective.
d. Providing training in early identification of MH disorders and risks excludes community staff in schools.

94. Which of the following is a primary benefit of professional learning communities?

a. They provide opportunities for teachers to share ideas.
b. They provide constructive feedback on student performance.
c. They identify areas in the curriculum that need revision.
d. They ensure that the standards-based curriculum is delivered.

95. Which of the following best represents a threat to a physically safe campus environment?

a. Inefficient arrival and dismissal procedures
b. High student-to-teacher classroom ratios
c. High teacher turnover
d. Electrical hazards

96. The campus testing coordinator has noticed that many of the teachers have been casual about following testing procedures when administering standardized tests to students. The testing coordinator knows that failure to adhere to testing procedures could result in consequences for individual staff members, the campus, or even the students. What next step should the testing coordinator take to address this concern?

a. Conduct training to address common testing procedure violations.
b. Send an email to staff warning them of the potential consequences if they violate testing procedures.
c. Modify the campus testing plan to omit teachers who are likely to commit testing violations.
d. Maintain documentation of violations in the event of an audit.

97. Which of the following is an example of a community partnership?

a. Student club members pick up litter in the community on the weekends.
b. A local business sets up a table at parent meetings to inform parents about their services.
c. Local businesses provide mentors to students in the areas of business and entrepreneurship.
d. The principal invites a local business owner as a guest speaker for a teacher in-service.

98. Which of the following actions taken by a principal best addresses the problem of having primarily novice teachers on staff?

a. Increased teacher observations and feedback
b. Facilitating collaborative and team teaching
c. Monitoring data closely
d. Providing tutorials for students after school

99. A principal notices that even though teachers actively participate in professional development throughout the school year, there seems to be little evidence of changes in instructional practices on campus. Which of the following questions best addresses the concern of the principal?

a. What is the process for giving feedback on the efficacy of professional development offered to teachers?
b. Are professional development sessions aligned to the curriculum, instruction, and programs of this campus?
c. How much does professional development impact the school budget?
d. How can I make time in my schedule to attend professional development sessions with the teachers?

100. What does research into school mental health show about collaboration with the community?

a. Clinical psychiatric care and other services are not practicable or suitable in schools.
b. A cohesive continuum of intervention must primarily address severe mental health problems.
c. School staff must work with families and service providers rather than policymakers.
d. An integrated intervention continuum must mainly address universal student need.

101. A school leader has recently been appointed to school principal of ABC Elementary School. Which of the following actions would best help the new principal learn more about the community that the school serves?

a. Research the community online.
b. Review student demographic and academic performance data.
c. Meet with a variety of stakeholders of the community.
d. Meet with current staff to ask questions about the community.

102. What is the primary reason that curriculum and instruction must be aligned to assessments?

a. School leaders must be able to justify why they select curriculum and resources.
b. Teachers must know what to teach in the classroom.
c. Assessments that are not aligned with curriculum and instruction will not accurately measure what students learned.
d. Alignment of curriculum and assessments makes it easier to analyze and compare student performance data.

103. The dean of instruction is preparing to implement an online literacy program that the school district has just purchased. Which feature of the literacy program platform best aligns with the school's mission to use data to make instructional decisions?

a. The program assesses students' reading levels bi-weekly.
b. The program tracks students' growth over time and compares their actual growth to expected growth.
c. The program autogenerates reports of student engagement and sends them to parents.
d. The program provides all teachers and administrators with access to a data dashboard that includes all data collected through the program.

104. Which of the following pieces of information would be most relevant when determining how to differentiate instruction for students?

a. Previous academic performance, special needs (such as a physical or learning disability), and learning style
b. Previous academic performance, demographics, and socioeconomic status
c. Student interests, career goals, and grade point average
d. Student interests, parental input, and learning style

105. Which of the following factors may directly affect a school leader's ability to recruit and retain highly qualified teachers?

a. The number of recruitment fairs that a school leader attends
b. The percentage of experienced teachers already on campus
c. The school culture
d. The available technology on campus

106. Which of the following sources and types of data would be best to use to provide feedback to teachers so that they can improve student learning?

a. Classroom observations, student class grades, and summative assessment data
b. Formative assessment data, attendance data, and behavior data
c. Classroom observations, survey data, and diagnostic testing data
d. Formative assessment data, diagnostic testing data, and projected performance data

107. According to some school consensus-building models, which of these is most typical?

a. One hundred percent of faculty must agree to implement what is proposed 100 percent of the time.
b. Dissenting members can opt out of the implementation.
c. If consensus seems impossible, having 80 percent of members agree is not enough.
d. Those dissenting must agree not to obstruct and to support implementation.

108. A school leader is developing a plan for effective use of an annex building on the school property. Which of the following staff members would be able to best assist the school leader in developing this plan?

a. A lead teacher
b. The plant operator
c. An assistant principal
d. The district superintendent

109. What is most true about effective new teacher induction programs?

a. They should focus on supporting new teachers but not leaders.
b. They should give only new teachers professional development.
c. They should use self-assessments and reflection for teachers to measure performance.
d. They should improve student achievement via teacher efficacy.

110. Which of the following is the best way that a school leader can ensure equitable treatment of students and staff?

a. Develop policies and procedures and adhere to them.
b. Create advisory committees with representatives from a variety of diverse demographics.
c. Create a diversity and inclusion statement for the school.
d. Address student and staff complaints swiftly.

111. Fire code regulations mandate that a fire drill should be conducted on campus monthly. It is the last day of the month and the principal realizes that a fire drill has not yet been conducted for the month. However, students are taking a mock standardized assessment. What action should the principal take?

a. Conduct the fire drill immediately.
b. Contact the fire inspector and inform them that the school was unable to conduct a fire drill for the month.
c. Document why the fire drill was not conducted for the month and provide the documentation if requested.
d. Contact the fire inspector to request an exception for the month.

112. A school leader has decided to hire an instructional coach to support the teachers' growth. Which of the following is the most likely result of this decision?

a. The instructional coach will help the leadership team supervise and evaluate teachers.
b. The instructional coach will make the decisions regarding professional development and training on campus.
c. Having an instructional coach will eliminate the need for professional development and training on campus.
d. The instructional coach will provide individualized support to teachers to help them grow.

113. Which of the following is an accurate statement about tiered behavior management systems used with classrooms and/or individual students?

a. Classroom behavior management systems should start at the beginning of the school year.
b. Individual programs for disruptive student behavior must start at the beginning of the school year.
c. Classroom behavior management systems are applied for a school year, not across grades.
d. If students know expectations early on, then classroom management systems can be faded.

114. What is the primary purpose of professional learning communities?

a. To hold teachers accountable
b. To make it easier to monitor teaching and learning
c. To facilitate collaboration among teachers
d. To set and achieve instructional goals

115. Which of the following best represents a threat to an emotionally safe campus environment?

a. Bullying
b. Crowded classrooms
c. High teacher turnover
d. High rates of student suspensions

116. A school leader is developing a process for continuous improvement on campus. Which of the following actions should the school leader take first?

a. Develop evaluation procedures and set checkpoints for evaluation.
b. Train staff on the continuous improvement process.
c. Select a low performing area that needs to be addressed.
d. Identify strategies for addressing low performing areas.

117. A school leader conducts a data review and realizes that the school will not meet an important milestone in the action plan for accomplishing one of the school goals. Which of the following actions should be taken first?

a. Begin developing a revised action plan.
b. Communicate goal progress with the appropriate stakeholders to identify the barriers and challenges that prevented the milestone from being met.
c. Identify who was responsible for the failure and offer corrective action.
d. Host a community meeting to share an update with all stakeholders.

118. Which of the following actions best demonstrates that a school leader is open to changing positions on an issue?

a. The school leader lets staff vote on decisions.
b. The school leader has an advisory committee made up of teachers, students, and community members.
c. The school leader holds regular community meetings to provide updates on school activities.
d. The school leader makes time to take phone calls from parents outside of school hours.

119. A group of community members meet with the principal to share concerns that the community does not believe the principal is effectively communicating data about progress toward the school vision and goals. The community members explain that many of them are not able to attend meetings held at the school. Which of the following solutions should the principal suggest to the community members?

a. Change the dates and times that community meetings are held so that more people can attend.
b. Have community members who attend the meetings inform others who did not attend about what was discussed at the meeting.
c. Refer community members to the school website where the meeting minutes are posted.
d. Develop a variety of ways to communicate in addition to the community meetings, such as via email, a school newsletter, and regular phone calls.

120. The technology teacher informs the school leader that the computers in the computer lab are outdated and make it difficult to provide technology instruction to students. What action should the principal take first?

a. Ask the technology teacher to choose a computer model to purchase to replace the outdated computers.
b. Allocate money in the budget to purchase new computers for the computer lab.
c. Refer to the campus technology plan to identify the timeline for replacing computers in the lab.
d. Request a district technology support staff member to service the computers in the computer lab.

Constructed Response

1. You are the principal of an 1800-student urban high school with a primarily African-American and Hispanic/Latino student population. The school has an active student newspaper with a much-beloved journalism teacher. Over the past several months, the student-staff have published several items of dubious origin that have caused controversy in the larger community. These items have typically had topics dealing with race relations. You have spoken to the journalism teacher after each incident about not allowing students to publish this type of questionable content. The newest issue of the student newspaper contains another such item. In 150-300 words, describe what you would do to address the situation.

2. You are the new principal of a 700-student elementary (K-5) school. The previous principal left the school in the midst of some controversy and there has been a significant turnover in teaching staff. In your first couple of weeks on the job, you notice a considerable amount of negativity among staff, in large part fomented by teachers who have been at the school for several years and have had multiple principals. In 300-600 words describe the strategies that you would use to address this negativity and change the culture of the school to a more positive tone and improve teacher and staff morale.

3. A group of parents have become increasingly disruptive at basketball games at the high school where you are the principal. There has been swearing, yelling, derogatory comments, etc. from the home bleachers. In 150-300 words, discuss how this situation could escalate, causing serious problems for the school, and outline the steps you would take to prevent this from happening.

4. Daisy Elementary School has recently seen a rise in the population of its immigrant students. Located in a socioeconomically disadvantaged community, most of its 653 students are from single-parent households or have parents that both work long hours. Many students' families have limited or no English language proficiency skills.

Teachers and staff at Daisy Elementary have traditionally had a difficult time encouraging students' families to participate in the school community. Many report trying to communicate with families via phone or email with little response. With continuously declining school-wide achievement on standardized assessments, Ms. Bryan, the school principal, believes that increasing family engagement in the education program will be beneficial in improving students' scores. Although she leads monthly Parent Teacher Association meetings, attendance is often low. At the most recent meeting, she discussed strategies for increasing family engagement with the few attendees. Ms. Bryan has also asked teachers to begin keeping communication logs in order to begin analyzing correlations between types of family communication and response rates. With this information, she intends to develop a plan for increasing family participation in the school community, and ultimately, improving student achievement.

Task:

Read the documents below. Then, write a response in which you:

- Identify two possible causes for low family participation in the school community
- Discuss the correlation between family engagement in the education program and student achievement
- Discuss two strategies that should be included in a plan for increasing family engagement
- Explain why the strategies you identified would be effective for this purpose

Documents

- Student demographics and assessment score statistics
- Minutes from the most recent Parent Teacher Association Meeting
- Excerpt from one teacher's family communication log
- Teacher communication/family response rate statistics

Student Demographic Statistics

Student Identifier	Percent of School Population
Students receiving free or reduced meals	84%
English Language Learner (ELL)	72%
Immigrant Students	78%
Students with Disabilities	8%

Student Test Score Statistics

Percentage of Passing Students (ELA & Mathematics Standardized Assessments)

School Year	All Students	Low SES Students	ELL Students	Immigrant Students	Students with Disabilities
2016-2017	70	58	56	60	82

School Year	All Students	Low SES Students	ELL Students	Immigrant Students	Students with Disabilities
2017-2018	57	41	54	58	80
2018-2019	52	34	48	51	75
2019-2020	41	30	37	44	74
2020-2021	36	28	30	32	67

Excerpt of Minutes from Most Recent Parent Teacher Association Meeting

Daisy Elementary School – Parent Teacher Association Meeting

Monday, October 4th, 2021

Discussion Agenda:

- Review student assessment scores from last year
- Curriculum review
- Family engagement strategies
- Family concerns/questions

Meeting Minutes:

- Attending family members had several questions about the implications of assessment score data. Many were unaware of how their children performed on ELA and Math assessments last year.
- Conflicting schedules, lack of time, and limited opportunities for participation were cited as reasons for low family engagement.
- We discussed how to schedule classroom visits and observations. Many family members were unaware that they could visit their child's classroom.
- Family members reported receiving little communication from teachers.
- We reviewed the curriculum for the year and discussed academic benchmarks for each grade level. Families were shown how to access this curriculum on the school's website.

Excerpt of one teacher's communication log

Teacher: Ms. Nelson Grade: 4th Class size: 28

Date	Student Family Member	Type/Purpose of Communication	Response?
August 30	All	Email- Welcome back to school	Four parents responded
September 3	All	Email – Weekly updates	One parent responded asking about homework policy
September 10	All	Email- Student progress reports	No response
September 15	Mother of Kelly H.	Phone call – Behavior issue	No answer. Left a voicemail. No response.
September 17	All	Email – Student progress reports	No response.

Date	Student Family Member	Type/Purpose of Communication	Response?
September 20	All	Back-to-school night	Three parents attended. We discussed learning goals for the year and their children's interests.
September 22	Mother of Jason L.	Phone call – Requesting a conference to address academic concerns	No answer. Left a voicemail. No response.
September 24	All	Email – Student progress reports	One parent responded regarding concerns over their child's math grades
October 5	Mother of Michael S.	Email – Behavior issue	Mother responded. Said she will talk to him.
October 8	All	Email – Student progress reports	No response
October 12	Grandmother of Amy H.	Email – Behavior issue	No response
October 15	All	Email – Student progress reports	One parent responded regarding concerns over her daughter's science grade

Teacher Communication Statistics/Family Response Rates

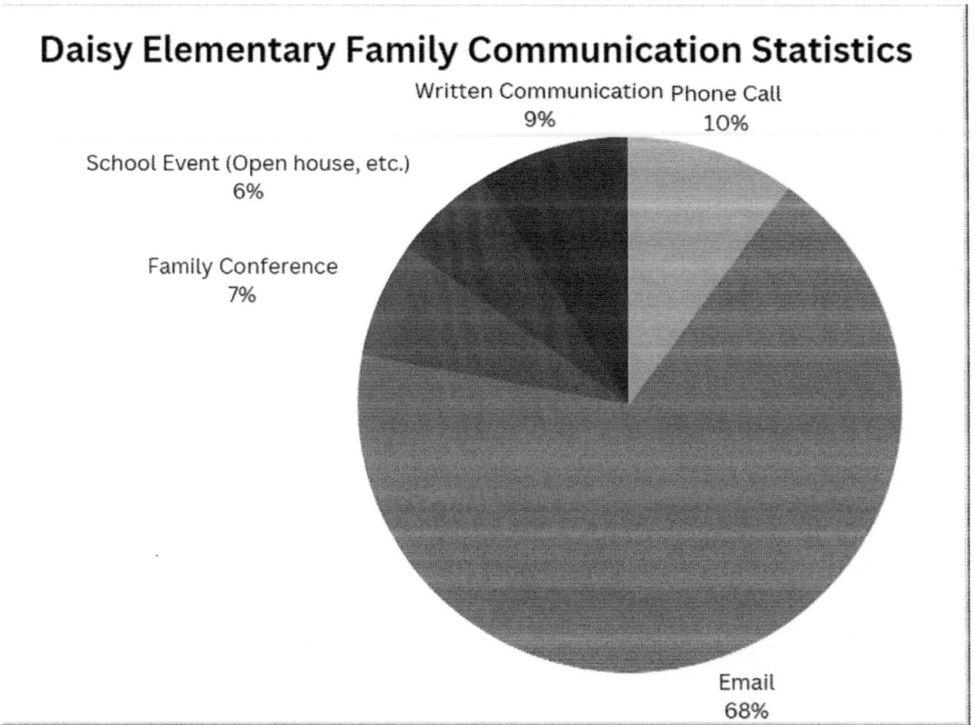

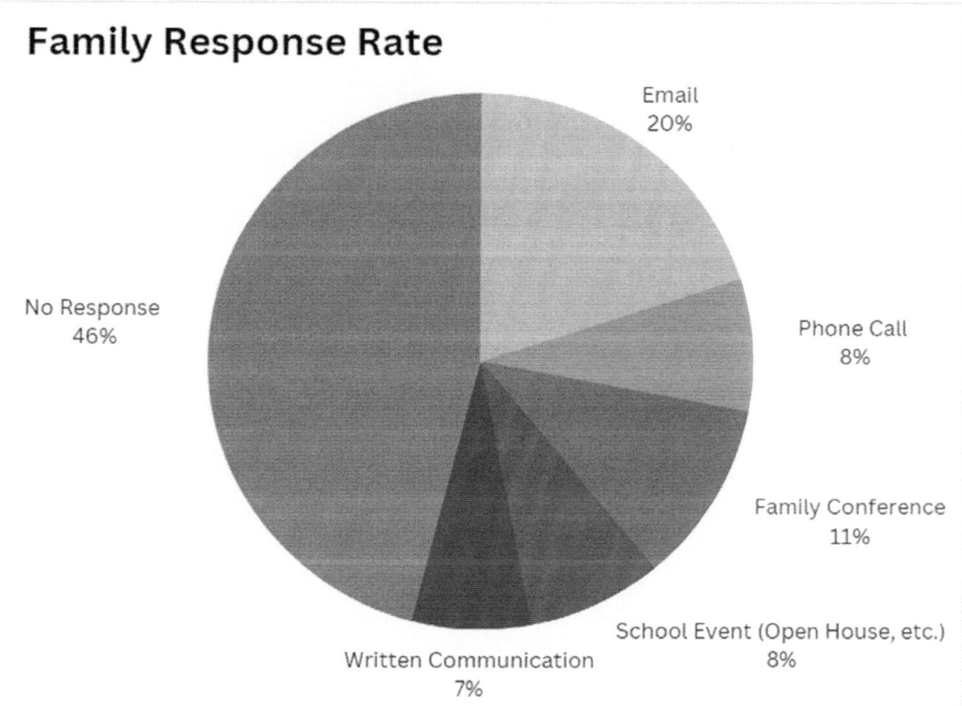
Family Response Rate
Email
20%
Phone Call
8%
Family Conference
11%
School Event (Open House, etc.)
8%
Written Communication
7%
No Response
46%

Answer Key and Explanations for Test #2

Selected-Response Questions

1. A: Data must be compared from one point in time to another to determine progress. Benchmark tests are typically used to assess objectives taught during a certain period and do not necessarily assess the same objectives from test to test; therefore, benchmark scores would not necessarily compare the same data to determine progress. Student portfolios from multiple marking periods would provide an assessment of authentic student performance over time and would be most helpful in determining student progress.

2. A: Classroom management systems, e.g., tiered school-wide positive behavior support systems, make learning environments orderly, enabling students to learn more easily and succeed academically. Rather than only controlling student behavior, they foster and sustain appropriate classroom behavior while also promoting student emotional and social development. They are effective for increasing both prosocial behavior and academic engagement in students. By providing universal supports in the first-tier school-wide, they succeed for 80-85% of students, while individualized intensive interventions are reserved for the remaining 15-20% in the third tier.

3. A: When a school leader attends a district school board meeting in an unfamiliar community, he or she is likely to encounter issues that were not prevalent in his previous community. If the school leader is receptive to change, he or she is likely to expand understanding of issues and grow as a school leader by experiencing a variety of perspectives. Seeing areas of disagreement (B) and seeing differences between district and school vision(D) can be helpful in addressing conflict and working to unify a school or district's vision, but is does not necessarily help develop the school leader's perspectives. Learning to run school board meetings (C) does not help with developing beliefs about educational issues.

4. D: Psychological disorders are usually the least addressable within a school context. Psychological disorders (D) are frequently biological, genetic, and chronic (potentially stemming from long-term stressors) and are LEAST likely to be caused by or treated effectively in a school setting. These typically require psychotherapeutic intervention and often treatment through therapy or medication. External stressors (A) can exist in the home, community, and/or school. Stressors are also generally considered an environmental challenge, meaning that changes in the environment can have an impact on the student's response. Educational problems (B) can originate within the individual student (such as a learning disability), family, community, and/or school-related factors. As such, schools often have resources to support students facing these challenges. Psychosocial problems (C) refers to a student experiencing psychological or emotional distress as a result of social factors. Psychosocial problems can often be addressed in schools by making changes to the social environment or through counseling.

5. B: Although the principal should be concerned with a variety of ways that this influx of students may impact the current instructional program, the primary concern should be how equipped the school is to provide this special population of students with an appropriate education. Human resources may include teachers and paraprofessionals. Fiscal resources may include furniture, equipment, technology, and other physical resources needed to support instruction.

6. B: A leader demonstrates shared leadership by assigning persons particular leadership responsibilities and granting them the authority to fulfill those leadership responsibilities. When sharing leadership, responsibilities are not dependent on job titles and can thus be delegated to any staff members who are capable of fulfilling the role. While sharing leadership can also involve including others in decision-making processes, shared leadership is best exemplified when a leader distributes power and authority to others.

7. C: Evaluating and revising campus-based assessments to ensure alignment to standards demonstrates a commitment to school-wide rigorous instruction. Assessments should accurately measure the standards. Increasing the offering of advanced placement and dual credit courses supports rigorous curriculum for some students who qualify, but does not impact rigor school wide. Similarly, increasing participation in college entrance exams does not raise the rigor of instruction on campus, but encourages students to seek and prepare for college admittance.

8. A: The school provides education and training to students that will make them employable in the community workforce. As a result, the school can supplement or adjust school programming to respond to the needs of the community, such as training students in particular employment fields that are experiencing a shortage within the community. Many schools, especially secondary schools, partner with their local community colleges and community organizations to identify employment trends in order to support the local community and increase the likelihood that graduates can obtain employment.

9. A: The primary benefit of evaluating staff members is to provide an opportunity for leaders to identify areas of strength and weakness among the staff and to provide constructive feedback to staff members so that they can grow professionally. Leaders can use these evaluations to determine what additional support and resources need to be provided to support or improve the performance of staff members.

10. D: Testing procedures may vary, but there are specific guidelines for reporting testing violations. The principal should report the alleged testing violation to the appropriate authorities so that it can be handled according to proper procedure. Confronting the accused teacher or attempting to investigate the allegation could impair the investigation. Documenting the complaint may be a step that the principal will need to take after the allegation has been reported per protocol.

11. C: For school professional development to meet student needs and achieve school goals best, it should be provided to all staff, not only to teachers, specialists, and other faculty or professionals. It should also be embedded in the job rather than separated, differentiated to address the individual challenge areas of teachers and other staff members, and provided on an ongoing basis instead of a periodic one.

12. C: The PLC will include teachers in the same grade level in different subjects which is horizontal alignment. The PLC will also include teachers in different grade levels in the same subject which is vertical alignment. Consequently, this PLC is an example of both horizontal and vertical alignment of curriculum and instruction.

13. D: All the choices are benefits of gathering the data, but the primary benefit is obtaining multiple sources of data to accurately identify the strengths, needs, gaps, and areas of improvement for the school. The school leader chose a combination of quantitative and qualitative data to accurately assess school performance and the cultures, values, attitudes, and beliefs that impact that performance. It is important to use data from multiple sources to develop the school vision and goals because using only one source of data may portray a limited or skewed picture of the school. Using multiple sources of data can confirm the validity of data and provide a more complete picture of the complex dynamics of a school campus.

14. D: An effective school leader is transparent when making decisions. This transparency includes sharing data and/or rationale for making decisions. The school leader has already determined that the fine arts program should be discontinued so the best action for the principal to take next is to explain the rationale for that decision to the school community.

15. A: The athletic director acted inappropriately by breaching confidential information. As a result, the drug testing plan will need to be revised and some level of disciplinary procedures should take place. This breach of information should be handled officially and documented in the event that more issues arise later on. The infraction is not a personal matter, but is one dealing with breach of policy, so this should be made into an official written reprimand (choice A), rather than as a note in a personnel file (choice B). Finally, assuming this is the first major offense by the athletic director, the offense is not likely to be so consequential that the athletic director should be removed from his or her position as in choice D.

16. D: Because research studies repeatedly prove student benefits of smaller class sizes, school leaders must hire and retain adequate human resources in terms of quantity and quality. For a safe, comfortable teaching and learning environment, school leaders must provide adequate physical resources like space, furniture, lighting, temperature control, etc. They must manage fiscal resources well to manage all other resources, not just some.

17. B: Recognizing and celebrating educational success is an effective strategy to develop positive family and community partnerships. A school leader should make an effort to organize events on campus and in the community to develop positive partnerships. Live events facilitate two-way communication, unlike newsletters which are one-way modes of communication. Attending athletic events and soliciting feedback from the community are additional ways to build a relationship with the community, but the most effective strategy for building a positive partnership is to host an event that spotlights positive things related to the school and students.

18. D: School principals should remain objective when observing teachers, regardless of their tenure or contract status. An evaluation rubric for teacher assessment should be used fairly and objectively for all teachers. A principal should observe what assignments the teacher gives the students, whether they are actively implementing new strategies, and the overall classroom environment and culture.

19. A: Student performance data is a valuable source of data for determining teacher efficacy. Effective instruction should result in student academic growth and satisfactory performance. Survey data and self- assessments can inform support and professional development for teachers but are not as useful in teacher evaluations due to their qualitative and subjective nature.

20. A: Leaders should use as many opportunities as possible to observe staff performance in order to have a well-rounded view of their performance. The opportunities may include various days of the week, times of the day, and varied circumstances. A leader should be intentional and deliberate about seeking different opportunities to observe staff at a variety of times in a variety of circumstances in order to obtain a fair and holistic view of staff performance.

21. B: While staying informed of new trends and technology is useful in this role, it is not central to the actual implementation of a new technology that is in its early implementation. Change management often requires more direct support of a wide range of needs from staff and students. Demonstrating the use of the technology (choice A), setting expectations and encouraging effort (choice C), and helping with implementation (choice D) all are a more direct way the school leader should help to implement change in this situation. Both question and answer are highlighted.

22. D: Educators should base their education practices on research-based practices with proven results. These practices are outlined in peer-reviewed research and texts based on this type of research. Additionally, the Department of Education reports on the efficacy of educational programs, products, practices, and policies through the What Works Clearinghouse. Educators should prioritize educational practices that have been proven to be effective before implementing practices based on personal experience or experimentation that is often a component of action research.

23. A: Rigor in academic instruction refers to curriculum and instruction that is challenging to students. Rigorous instruction challenges students academically, but also intellectually and even personally. Rigorous instruction is often complex and challenges students to think deeply and critically. Rigor does not mean excessively hard or difficult. However, rigor does involve instruction that is stimulating and engaging. Rigorous instruction often requires students to make connections across academic content areas and apply concepts to the real world.

24. A: A school leader must develop a plan for assessing and monitoring progress toward established goals. When monitoring is done consistently, the school leader will be aware of whether the school is meeting, exceeding, or falling short of established goals in a timely manner. Regularly monitoring progress toward goals will allow the school leader opportunity to make corrections in the strategies and implement actions, if needed.

25. D: Hiring a coach that can train teachers to use differentiated instruction and evaluate them for efficacy would be the most effective strategy for increasing the uses of differentiated instruction on campus. An instructional coach can provide individual and collective support and can monitor and encourage continuous implementation of the strategy. Praising teachers who implement differentiated instruction creates a positive climate but does not help teachers who do not know how to implement differentiated instruction to do so. Similarly, providing resources and modeling are not sufficient actions to take to increase the use of differentiated instruction if teachers do not know how to implement it or do not see the benefit in implementing the strategy.

26. C: According to the Collaborative for Academic, Social, and Emotional Learning (CASEL), effective SEL programs incorporate sequenced and systematic programming across all grade levels, monitor the programming continuously, offer opportunities for students to practice the skills they learn, and coordinate school environments with community environments.

27. C: It is most important for the school leader to identify the appropriate staff to manage the physical plant. This staff member has the primary responsibility to ensure the safe functioning of everything on campus; therefore, the leader must choose the right staff member for the job and monitor the performance of that staff member. While it is important for the school leader to personally inspect their campus on a regular basis, management of the physical plant must be delegated to an appropriate staff member to ensure that the campus is maintained appropriately.

28. C: The DOJ collaborated with the ED in producing a positive school discipline guidance package as part of the SSDI to prevent or reduce student movement from schools to justice and correctional systems, not match school discipline to practices in those systems; replace disciplinary exclusion with better alternatives, rather than regard student justice involvement as inevitable and wait to address that; ensure Titles IV and VI of the Civil Rights Act prohibiting discrimination are enforced, which is the DOJ's job; and establish fair disciplinary practices to keep all students in school, not exclude any.

29. C: School leaders must ensure in advance that most that the specific responsibilities of each member of the command and control group are clearly defined for a variety of different crisis situations. Tenure is not an equitable way of selecting members. Distributing leadership could cause confusion during a crisis, and a complex reporting system could defeat the whole purpose of such a team.

30. C: Most school expenditures are related to classroom instruction. These expenditures include teacher salaries, libraries, professional development for teachers, curriculum development, and instructional technology. Operations is the next highest percentage of budgetary expenditures, followed by administration and student support services. Student support services involve expenses such as social work, guidance, health expenses, and psychological services.

31. C: To encourage teacher leadership, school leaders must create safe environments wherein teachers can take risks and think creatively. School leaders should share authority with teachers to assist them in developing leadership skills and demonstrate responsibility. Increasing a teacher's workload with work that is not directly related to increased responsibilities or to skill refinement is not an example of developing a teacher. Additionally, leaders must differentiate support for teachers based on the current performance, skill, and attitudes.

32. C: Shared leadership, regular monitoring of progress, and accountability of everyone participating in implementation are key elements to consistent goal implementation. Sharing leadership creates buy in for the vision and empowers others to take action so that the leader is not solely responsible for making progress toward the vision. Regular monitoring of goal progress using milestones and timelines keeps everyone on pace for implementing the goals and vision. The leader must also hold people accountable because each person must do their part in order for the plan to be implemented successfully and according to schedule.

33. D: All curriculum and resources should be aligned to standards. Therefore, if standards change, it is likely that the curriculum will need to be revised and new resources purchased. However, before changes in the curriculum can be made, the principal will need to know how the new standards differ from the previous standards. This will help the principal determine if minor revisions to the curriculum are needed or if a new curriculum will need to be adopted.

34. D: Although the other sources of information can be helpful, the principal must ensure that all funds allotted in the school budget are aligned with the campus vision and goals. When school funds are utilized, there must be a return on the investment that aligns with the vision and goals for the school. Programs and resources that do not align with the school vision and goals must be deprioritized or even eliminated.

35. B: External stressors can create short-term or long-term obstacles for student learning and achievement and can lead to or be evidence of mental health issues. Not all student mental health issues or crises carry an official diagnosis; however, educators can provide support and resources for the symptoms that students display. Furthermore, students with diagnosed mental health issues may be provided support and resources through a 504-education plan in addition to or in lieu of an individualized education plan. Additionally, educators can offer resources and support to students with mental health issues who do not receive services under either program.

36. D: Effective curricular programs will help students grow academically. Meeting academic performance standards may not be a good indicator of appropriate curricular programs if there is a population of students on campus who are consistently exceeding the performance standards on assessments. Meeting only minimum standards would be a cause of concern and these students would need a curricular program that extends their learning and supports their academic growth. In contrast, an effective curricular program would foster academic growth for all students.

37. A: According to some education experts (cf. WestEd.org), school principals and districts surveyed across the United States have reported generally positive impressions of standards-based accountability systems, saying these have improved curriculum and instruction, student assessment practices (C), and student expectations and achievement. However, many districts (over 40%) also reported that teacher morale had been adversely affected by accountability pressures.

38. A: School-wide positive behavior support programs typically have three tiers. In tier 1, all students receive universal instructional and behavioral supports and interventions, which are effective for the majority. In tier 2, a minority of students needing more behavior support receive small-group instruction in academic subjects and emotional and social skills. In tier 3, an even smaller minority not responding to tier 2 interventions receives intensive, individualized interventions.

39. B: Participating in school- and district-sponsored events is not always the same as engaging with the greater community. Community stakeholders can include members of the community who do not have children enrolled in the school district but are contributors to the community as a whole. These stakeholders may include business owners, community organization leaders, and residents near the school. Additionally, community engagement involves opportunities for two-way communication between the school leader and community members. Attending the community parade gives the school leader an opportunity to represent the school at a community event and engage with community stakeholders. This increases the school leader's visibility in the community and demonstrates that the school is a part of the community that it serves.

40. A: Formative data helps teachers to assess their effectiveness during instruction (rather than after) and accordingly make adjustments to improve student outcomes. Summative data can assist teachers in identifying areas of improvement in their teaching practice but is often too late to identify specific remedial student groups. Student profiles from permanent records (e.g., demographics, assessment histories, family information, etc.) provide less detailed information to inform instruction. Enrollment data helps educators identify budgetary needs and student demographic distributions, but do not inform instruction, staff development, remedial student groups, or information plans.

41. C: The use of school funds represents a common ethical situation. All school funds should be used according to policies and procedures outlined by the school board. Using school funds for personal use is a violation of ethics.

42. B: There are times when the school leader will need to effectively communicate with the media for both positive and negative reasons. The school leader should first follow the protocols and procedures outlined by the school district when communicating with the media, especially in situations in which the media attention is negative for the school or district. Some school districts centralize media communication and do not permit school leaders or other staff to communicate with the media without express approval.

43. D: A school leader should focus on improving all teaching on campus, even teaching that is already considered effective. This reinforces a culture of high expectations on campus and demonstrates to high-performing teachers that they are valued. When a school leader is committed to improving all instruction on campus, even instruction that is considered effective, all staff are encouraged to grow professionally for the benefit of students.

44. B: Change in temperament or evasion of work, such as through frequent unexplained absences, are very strong indicators of a staff member who is stressed, feeling overwhelmed, or experiencing personal challenges. A change in work quality for a short term could be circumstantial, but over long periods of time, a decline in work quality could be an indicator of other factors such as mental health and stress. The school leader should recommend that the staff member take advantage of mental health and counseling resources that are available while respecting the staff member's privacy.

45. C: Parents and other community members must demand and support quality professional development (PD) that improves teaching, school leadership, and student achievement. School boards must hold educators accountable for results and provide policies clarifying that the purpose of PD is to enhance educator efficacy and thus student learning. Educators who organize and facilitate PD must understand which student learning needs they and their fellow educators have difficulty addressing. School system administrators must allot time and otherwise facilitate PD that will help educators address student learning problems.

46. B: Hazard analysis: analyzing food service operation and determining likely food safety hazards and control measures. Identifying CCPs: identifying those few control measures absolutely essential to food safety. Determining critical limits: cooking temperatures, times, and other observable and measurable safety-defining boundaries. Establishing CCP monitoring procedures: tracking CCP control as food flows through operations. Planning corrective actions: planning what to do when a critical limit at a CCP is not met and communicating to and training employees in preventive decisions. Verification procedures: ensuring a scientifically sound system for effective hazard control. Record-keeping system: documenting the HACCP system and plan.

47. C: The school leader's responsibility is to investigate the accusation that has been made to determine next steps. An investigation is needed because the school leader cannot take immediate action in response to the teachers' actions based solely on the report of the parent. Whether the teachers will be disciplined or not, the school leader should not discuss such discipline of personnel with others.

48. B: Although there are many factors and influences outside of the school that can lead a young person to commit suicide, the school and its staff can serve as a resource and support for students who experience suicidal thoughts. A school leader should ensure that there are systems in place on campus that allow students to express their needs so that they can be referred for services. This may include having walk-in counseling hours or open-door policies with key staff members.

49. C: When scheduling parent meetings for large groups of parents, the school leader should consider the time of the day and the day of the week that these meetings are to be held. The goal of these meetings is to effectively communicate with parents in a group setting, so the school leader needs to ensure that the scheduled time and day of the meeting accommodates the majority of parents for maximum attendance.

50. A: The principal's announcement that they are committing to an ongoing training program indicates that they are committed to professional growth. This is a model to the other members of the leadership team.

51. D: An acceptable use policy is a document that dictates how students use the school's physical technology device, hardware, software, and Internet and network access. An acceptable use policy is a document that is usually signed to indicate that the user acknowledges the terms of technology use and understands the consequences of not abiding by those terms.

52. B: Of the strategies listed, the strategy that best addresses the achievement gap is providing targeted interventions to students who perform unsatisfactorily. Disaggregating data helps to identify the achievement gap, but does not address it. Tracking and projecting student performance also has the potential to identify the achievement gap, but does not address it. Rather than lowering standards, holding high expectations and standards helps to reduce the achievement gap.

53. D: Reducing the teachers' teaching styles is not a priority if the teacher is effective at achieving standards in the curriculum. Reducing variability in classrooms throughout the school tends to promote efficiency in purchasing, and in producing testing materials, since each department can use the same materials. This also could allow for benchmarking from class to class, which helps with pacing the curriculum throughout the year. Other procedures and policies, such as bathroom policies or electronic device policies can promote safety by making sure each student is accounted for.

54. B: The school leader can form a parent focus group in order to gather feedback and opinions on decisions to be made at the school. A focus group would allow multiple parents to participate and would foster two-way communication. Two-way communication allows both parties to participate and contribute. One-way communication methods can gather input from others or deliver information, but they do not allow stakeholders to actively participate in the decision-making process.

55. A: In diverse communities, school leaders often encounter language barriers when attempting to communicate with parents of students or other community members. While it is helpful when a school leader is fluent in more than one language, there are often a variety of languages that are spoken in these communities. There can be translators, including sign language interpreters, or translation machines available at community meetings when appropriate. There are also many businesses that offer translation services for documents and real-time translation for meetings and conferences.

56. A: This action best represents an effort to develop a culture of knowledge about and comfort with cultures other than the students' own. Whereas knowledge doesn't always have highly noticeable effects on the school culture in the short-term, it has long-term impact on the community because it helps to break down ignorance about other cultures. Students who know something about another culture are much more willing to interact with people from that culture, rather than avoid peers who are not like themselves. This is particularly helpful when implemented as a schoolwide policy rather than occurring in individual classes because it will have a greater impact on the entire culture of the school. Black History Month should be celebrated, but it only provides perspectives from one culture and doesn't necessarily encourage interaction between various cultures. Publishing a statement about diversity and inclusion likely does not show a strong enough gesture to encourage real change. Adding ASL to course offerings is also not likely to reach a broad enough audience to have a huge change, although it is great to have those options available.

57. C: Researchers have identified a number of transformational school leader practices promoting organizational staff learning, and the most effective transformational leaders best promote organizational learning by modeling ongoing learning in their own practices and affording staff opportunities to learn from peers. Demonstrating their high expectations for both students and teachers is important, but not necessarily central to organizational learning. While researching effective instructional practices and training staff on implementation is also useful, this approach is less aligned with transformational leadership.

58. A: When a school leader has clearly and effectively communicated the school vision and goals, others will be able to describe them in their own words. They will be able to communicate the vision and goals to others and explain the rationale behind them. Stakeholders who understand the vision and goals will propose ideas and actions that are aligned to the vision and will understand how they can participate in or contribute to achieving the vision.

59. A: All students receiving perfect scores for 18 consecutive weeks may be an indication that the students are not receiving rigorous curriculum and instruction. While there is an expectation for students to be successful in the classroom, there is low statistical likelihood that all students would perform perfectly over extended periods of time if they were receiving instruction at or above their level. Each student should receive a rigorous curriculum which means delivering instruction at an appropriate level of challenge in order to grow students academically.

60. A: A school leader should evaluate technology data systems used in the school by how well they provide relevant data for decision making. Affordability and whether other schools are using the data system are important questions to ask when considering purchasing a data system but are less relevant when evaluating the system after use. User friendliness is not as important in evaluation if training and support are readily available to staff who will use the data system.

61. C: Creating a grief counseling group in response to the death of a student is a positive action, but is reactive, not proactive. An education leader cannot predict every occurrence that may impact student mental and emotional health, but the education leader can create processes and structures that can support students ongoing emotional safety. These can include designing referral systems for mental health care, providing information about available resources to students and their parents, and using school resources to provide mental health support.

62. B: The disproportionate number of students suspended from school based on race may indicate that there are beliefs influencing how teachers relate to students. The school principal needs to identify if there is evidence of this in the school culture and whether campus policies perpetuate negative beliefs.

63. A: A school leader must identify key stakeholders within the school community, including those with competing perspectives. The school leader should meet with the group of disgruntled teachers, also, to facilitate two-way communication. The school leader will have an opportunity to listen to and address the group members' concerns, while the teachers will have an opportunity to hear the rationale for certain policies and procedures.

64. D: Different roles on campus can help accomplish the vision. The school leader can ensure the success of the school vision by engaging the internal community and including diverse perspectives in the implementation of the vision. This strategy increases buy in and utilizes staff members' roles to accomplish the vision. For example, the administrative team can lead projects and delegate tasks to others, school counselors can support the psychosocial needs of students to support their academic success, teacher leaders can lead and support the instructional staff, and support staff can support the logistics and communication of the plans.

65. A: Lack of family and community involvement is typically not a result of parents and others being uninterested in students' learning, working with educators, or influencing students' futures. It is more likely the result of unrealistic educator attitudes in expecting parents and others to seek involvement independently, and some educator methods are ineffective, like posting fliers at school when parents rarely visit, sending them home with students who forget to give them to parents, etc. Experts find educator efforts must be more intensive and organized to involve families and communities.

66. A: All staff can benefit from diversity training so they can challenge any negative assumptions that they may have about various populations of students or staff. School leaders must take caution not to allow negative assumptions and beliefs to impact the hiring process or the implementation of policies and procedures on campus.

67. A: To realize instructional change over time, professional development (PD) must be provided on an ongoing basis and reinforced through repetition and classroom follow-up activities. Teachers need theoretical understanding not only of the theory underling instructional practices, but also of how they can apply theory to practice. PD is best administered as a component of a comprehensive, systematic, district-supported educational reform process. When school leaders furnish PD, they should be careful to avoid topics lacking research support, unrelated to student learning, and popular new fads.

68. D: It is beneficial to the school community, the community at large, and postsecondary education institutions to align education expectations between secondary school and postsecondary school. The communication between postsecondary institutions and school leaders can help identify the skills necessary to succeed in college, trends in degree programs, and career paths. This type of communication can also lead to the integration of higher education programming on school campuses, such as dual-credit enrollment or training and certification programs.

69. D: Schools and communities benefit mutually from school leader outreach. For example, community partners become better informed about school functions and needs and develop a sense of ownership in the school. They appreciate and remember the invitations, acknowledgements, and thanks of school leaders. School leaders show they recognize their school belongs to the community by offering community access to school facilities for various events, benefiting not only the community but also the school when community members gain better understandings of the school and its positive effects on student lives.

70. B: The best way to ensure that others are acting ethically is to actively monitor employee behavior. This can be done in person by walking around and observing performance, instructing others on the leadership team to observe employee behavior, and monitoring using security cameras. Security cameras are useful in areas that are most prone to unethical conduct, such as places where money is exchanged, entrances and exits, records storage, and areas on campus that are not frequently trafficked. While it is recommended to have policies and procedures for ethical behavior in place, the school leader must actively monitor adherence to those policies and procedures.

71. D: Measurable goals can be quantified, and non-measurable goals cannot be quantified. This goal is measurable because calculating the percentage of students who earned at least a B average in their math class can reveal whether or not the goal was met. It also identifies how students are expected to perform in order to reach the goal. When goals are measurable, it is easy to determine whether or not the goal has been met.

72. A: The components of an effective plan include action steps, persons responsible, time frames, milestones, resources needed, and evidence of implementation. The plan will include the resources needed to accomplish the plan so that these resources are planned for and obtained, thus preventing delay in the plan's accomplishment. The evidence of implementation should be included in the plan so that ongoing monitoring can take place. Depending on the aspect of the plan, evidence of implementation could include documents, visible indicators, or regular meetings.

73. B: Students having family issues, or personal problems whose treatment involves family, are referred to family counselors. Group counseling promotes social skills and healthy interaction and can be provided within the school environment when the groups are selected with intention. Career counselors can help students choose career paths and preparation. Career counseling is often performed in schools by guidance counselors and others, making referrals infrequent.

74. D: The principal should take action that allows stakeholders to participate in the process of refocusing attention to campus vision and goals. A community meeting would allow for two-way communication so that the principal can hear the concerns of the community and so that the community can hear about the alignment of the program to the campus vision and goals.

75. A: Implementing differentiated instruction helps teachers to meet students where they are based on performance, learning style, and other student characteristics. Instruction can be differentiated based on lesson delivery, student activities, and student assessment. However, standards are often standardized and must remain the same for students as all students are expected to learn and succeed. Teachers can provide individualized resources and support to help students to meet those needs.

76. D: Attending a mandated training session indicates that the leader failed to identify that the training was needed for themselves, but instead needed to be directed by someone else to attend. Self-reflection involves reflecting on one's own performance in comparison to a set of leadership expectations and standards.

77. D: All of these factors are important to consider, but the leader must first ensure that the professional development will help staff meet the vision and goals that have already been established. A leader needs to be deliberate in selecting professional development for staff members so that the professional development is purposeful in helping staff achieve the campus goals and vision.

78. C: When a person finds value and worth in each student, they exemplify the educational philosophy that all students can learn. Some students may need more support or different resources, but they still have the capacity to learn. This teacher's statement that the student would fail anyway is in direct opposition to this philosophy.

79. B: The principal noted that they were not able to implement plans properly because they did not have time. Action items in the plan were not accomplished, indicating that this is a time management issue and the leader needs to set appropriate priorities for accomplishing tasks. Simply adding hours to one's work week does not mean that those hours will be spent completing the right tasks. School leaders must become efficient at prioritizing their activities to achieve school goals. Additionally, the leader is concerned with self-improvement, so holding others accountable is not an appropriate solution in this instance.

80. C: The school board elects or hires and supervises the superintendent, who in turns hires and supervises the school principal. In the hierarchy of public education leadership, the school board makes policy decisions based on state and local legislature and the superintendent implements these policies. School principals apply these policies to the daily operations of the school. There may be instances in which a principal participates in a school board meeting, such as by reporting data or speaking, but these activities are not part of the regular responsibilities of a principal in relation to the school board.

81. A: The best strategy the principal can use to establish a continuous improvement cycle is to assess students at regular intervals and adjust instruction based on the data. Benchmark exams are typically shorter assessments over selected objectives rather than large comprehensive assessments. Data from these assessments reflect the mastery of objectives that are recently taught and are aligned to the pacing of the curriculum scope and sequence. Testing in less frequent intervals can also be helpful if the data is used to adjust instruction immediately rather than informing plans for the subsequent school year.

82. A: Each of the suggestions are viable options for the school leader to implement; however, the school leader needs to know why teachers leave or plan to leave in order to best address the problem. Seeking feedback from the teaching staff can help the school leader to focus resources on the most direct causes of teacher attrition. Once the causes are identified, the school leader can determine if the other suggestions are applicable.

83. A: Data showing school improvement goals that are behind schedule indicate a need to update the school improvement plan—either by adjusting completion time criteria if school leaders and staff determine they were unrealistic in either case, or by adjusting instruction to be more effective if they determine current methods are delaying progress.

84. B: Although a technology budget cut is bad news, the principal would want to assess the current technology equipment on campus first. If the campus is already technology rich, the budget cut may not result in a drastic impact to instruction for the upcoming school year and little to no action may be necessary. After assessing the current technology equipment on campus, the principal can determine if the equipment meets the needs for the upcoming school year and, if not, how to make adjustments.

85. A: A leader effectively monitors goal progress by implementing clear checkpoints and milestones for goal activities. Each goal should be broken down into smaller goals, or milestones, that can be reviewed at regular intervals. This allows the leader to analyze progress toward the goal on a timeline so that if there is not sufficient progress toward the goal, there is time to intervene and make changes to the action steps.

86. D: Behavioral codes of conduct govern student, faculty, staff, and visitor behavior in schools. State regulations typically require schools to give teachers copies upon adoption, send all parents summaries before school years start, and give students copies when school years begin. However, to gain stakeholder buy in and to assure collective understanding and agreement, conduct codes can be developed jointly by parents, teachers, and students.

87. C: Whereas the National Association of Secondary School Principals (NASSP) recommends staff training in all these areas, strategies promoting school-wide positive environments are most related to Response to Intervention (RtI). RtI involves instituting school-wide positive learning and behavioral supports with three tiers of progressively more intensive intervention. Whereas the first tier includes universal screening, which relates to early identification (A), all three tiers benefit from school-wide positive supports, including students in Tiers 2 and 3, who receive additional interventions. Referrals (B) are only made for students not responding in Tier 3 and/or responding but needing additional services. Cooperative school models (D)are beneficial irrespective of using or not using RtI.

88. C: According to principles of adult learning, adults learn best in more informal formats rather than how children learn by following a formal curriculum. They prefer guidance and choices rather than directive instruction. Both children and adults learn by doing, but active, hands-on participation is even more important for adult learning. Adults want to learn practical information they need and can use immediately in their work rather than theoretical concepts.

89. B: Change is often opposed when stakeholders feel that the change is done without their consent and is outside of their control. As a result, obtaining stakeholder buy in can help make changes more effective. Goals should align to the changes but this strategy by itself will not help to manage the change. Additional training will be ineffective if stakeholders are opposed to the change. School leaders should listen to those who are opposed to the change and attempt to address their concerns rather than removing them from campus.

90. D: Letters and automated calls are acceptable forms of communication, but communication is most effective when parents and community members have the opportunity to engage in two-way conversation. Hosting a meeting gives participants a chance to ask questions and provide feedback to school leadership.

91. D: Many school districts require parents to provide express permission for their child to appear in photographs and videos for media purposes. Other school districts indicate that consent is implied unless there is written documentation expressly forbidding their child to appear in content for media. In either circumstance, the school leader needs to confirm that each student who will participate has permission from a parent or guardian to do so.

92. D: If possible, the school leader should communicate directly with the student and their family to learn about the student's academic, social, and emotional needs. Schools and school districts have policies and procedures for supporting students whose first language is not English so that these students can receive the support that they need to be academically successful. It is unlikely feasible to actually have a permanent translator available for all classes as in choice C, so a better first step is to start with a consultation using a translator temporarily while a plan is made.

93. C: Among many others, NASSP recommendations for promoting student mental health (MH) include providing comprehensive staff development\not only to school employees, but also to community service personnel working in the school; training school and community staff working in the school in promoting school-wide positive environments, which is found effective; training school staff in using referral mechanisms to help students access community MH services; and training both school and community staff working in schools in early identification of MH disorders and risks for these.

94. D: One of the foundations of a professional learning community is identifying the standards and curriculum that must be taught and ensuring that the curriculum is delivered effectively. A question that PLC members must ask is "What do we want students to learn?". Answering this question ensures that the standards-based curriculum is prioritized, and that formative and summative assessment is a reflection of the curriculum that is taught.

95. D: A physically safe environment is free from dangers, both seen and unseen, that would pose a threat to the physical safety of anyone exposed to the environment. A physically safe environment is in good repair, accessible to all, and accommodating in relation to the nature in which the environment is designated for use.

96. A: Widespread testing violations indicates that the staff would benefit from additional training regarding testing procedures. There may be misconceptions or gaps in information that may need to be addressed in the training.

97. C: Utilizing community services builds partnerships and relationships between the school and the community, which can have long-range benefits for both parties. When businesses provide mentors for students, they are engaged in activities over time that can have a positive impact on the school community.

98. B: Novice teachers need increased support. Facilitating collaboration between teachers and encouraging team teaching provides support for teachers while simultaneously improving the quality of instruction delivered to students. Monitoring data, conducting observations, offering feedback, and providing tutorials to students are beneficial actions, but are reactive to deficits in instruction. The principal is being proactive by facilitating collaborative teaching so that students will receive good instruction in the classroom.

99. B: The principal should determine which professional development sessions that teachers are attending and whether those sessions are aligned to the curriculum, instruction, and programs on campus. The professional development sessions may be informative but may not be practically applicable to the campus if they are not aligned with campus goals. For example, if a teacher attends a professional development session on project-based learning, yet the campus does not implement nor support project-based learning, there will be little to no evidence of changes in instructional practice on campus as a result of attendance to that session.

100. A: Research shows that, among others, one reason schools should collaborate with their communities to provide mental health services is that schools are not suitable settings for clinical psychiatric care and similar services. When collaborating with communities, school staff must work not only with families and community service providers, but also with policymakers to coordinate and connect needed support processes. A cohesive and integrated mental health intervention continuum must address both severe student problems and universal student needs.

101. C: Meeting with a diverse group of stakeholders from the community will give the new principal a well-rounded perspective of the community. Researching the community online, reviewing student data, and talking with staff are all effective methods of collecting information, but speaking directly with community members is a better source of more insightful information.

102. C: Curriculum and instruction must be aligned to assessment because what is taught must be measured and what is measured must be taught. If instruction is not aligned to the assessment, it is likely that there will be no measurement of how well students mastered what was taught. Additionally, if instruction is not aligned to the assessment, it is likely that students will be assessed on concepts and material that they have not been taught. Neither of the scenarios is fair or beneficial to students.

103. D: The online literacy program collects valuable data, but the data must be accessible by instructional decision makers for them to be able to make data-driven instructional decisions. Collecting data without being able to access it is not effective for data-driven decision making. In order for data to be useful, it must be easily accessible by those who need it in a timely manner. In this scenario, teachers and administrators would be able to access all the data in one location, which would facilitate using that data to make decisions using that data.

104. A: Differentiated instruction refers to providing customized or tailored instruction to students to meet their diverse learning needs. Previous academic performance, special needs (such as a physical or learning disability), and learning styles are good ways to determine how to differentiate instruction to meet student needs. Other sources of data, such as interests, career goals, and others can be helpful, but are not always relevant.

105. C: The school culture can create a welcoming environment for new teachers, or it can repel them. When the school culture is positive, focused on students, and driven by excellence, teachers will want to be a part of that culture. They will be motivated by the positive culture and will recruit others to join the team. On the other hand, if the school culture is negative, then teachers and staff will likely have negative attitudes as well. Teachers will seek a way out of that school environment rather than encouraging others to join the team. This negative culture can negatively affect students' academic performance and behavior. If a potential teacher candidate observes a negative school culture, they may be unwilling to work at that campus.

106. A: Classroom observations, student class grades, and summative assessment data would be the best sources of data to provide feedback to teachers to improve student learning. Data sources for improving teaching and learning should include instructional delivery (classroom observations) and student performance outcomes. Both formative and summative assessment data can be used to determine student mastery of objectives and efficacy of instructional delivery.

107. D: According to some school consensus-building models, although the ideal is for 100% of faculty members to agree to implement a recommendation, this is not always realistic and is not required 100% of the time. If consensus seems impossible, many schools have a rule stating that 80% of members agreeing is sufficient; dissenting members must promise not only to refrain from obstructing implementation, but furthermore to support it.

108. B: The plant operator oversees the operation of the school campus from a facilities standpoint. This staff member will have information related to the physical layout of the facility, its intended use, accessibility, and many other aspects of the physical building that will be helpful in determining how the building can be used appropriately.

109. D: Effective new teacher induction programs should focus on supporting not only the new teachers, but also the school leaders who guide them. This requires offering professional development not only to new teachers, but equally to their mentors, school leaders, and other site leaders. Effective induction programs use research-based and standards-based assessment instruments to assess and inform new teacher performance. The ultimate goal of teacher induction programs that make teachers more effective is to improve student achievement.

110. A: The best way that the school leader can ensure equitable treatment of students and staff is to develop policies and procedures and adhere to them. When there are policies and procedures in place, the school leader can refer to these to determine their course of action when dealing with students and staff. Policies and procedures help leaders proactively ensure that students and staff are treated equitably because they serve as guidelines for behavior and are not subjective. Creating an advisory committee can assist with developing these policies and procedures, but doing so does not shape the behavior of all staff and students. Additionally, while it is advisable that a school leader addresses student and staff complaints swiftly, this is a reactive response and likely occurs after someone has already been treated in an inequitable manner.

111. A: School leaders must abide by policies set forth by local safety departments. In this case, a fire drill may be disruptive to the school day, but it is a priority and must be conducted. In the future, the principal should plan when to conduct fire drills in advance rather than waiting and possibly failing to conduct them.

112. D: A coach is a professional who helps a teacher develop the skills necessary to do their job effectively. A coach is a staff member who does not supervise or evaluate the person being coached. This helps to foster a relationship of trust between the coach and the teacher. A coach will identify a teacher's areas of strength and weakness based on a predetermined rubric or set of expectations. Then the coach will provide one-on-one support to the teacher to help improve targeted areas. A coach may provide books and resources, recommend professional development sessions, model effective teaching methods, observe the teacher in practice to provide real-time feedback, assist in the lesson planning process, and guide the teacher in self-reflection and critical analysis processes. A coach provides individualized, targeted support to teachers and helps them to grow, usually in a shorter period of time than other forms of professional development support.

113. A: To be effective, research finds tiered behavior management systems applied at the classroom level should be established early in the school year; however, individual programs for disruptive student behaviors may begin at any time as needed. Classroom behavior management systems should be applied across the grades to give students consistent, ongoing input and reinforcement of procedures, rules, and expectations; and throughout the school year without fading to reinforce and support positive behavior.

114. C: Professional learning communities allow staff with shared roles or responsibilities to collaborate in a way that meets the needs of teachers and students. These communities are usually goal-driven and encourage the sharing of ideas and responsibilities. Professional learning communities are used in a variety of ways, but the primary purpose is to facilitate collaboration among educators.

115. A: An emotionally safe environment is an environment where everyone can learn. It is free from all obstacles, negative emotions, and conflicts due to preventative strategies and quick resolutions. When an environment is not emotionally safe, children can feel fear, anxiety, and a host of other negative emotions. In an emotionally safe environment, both adults and children feel comfortable participating in the learning environment and interacting with one another. There is an absence of peer-to-peer conflict, peer-to-adult conflict, and bullying.

116. A: The process of continuous improvement is the ongoing act of assessing performance and adjusting efforts in order to improve that performance. In order to implement a process of continuous improvement, there must be procedures of evaluation developed and implemented at regular checkpoints. Based on these regular evaluations, the leadership team can identify areas of improvement and initiate interventions and actions based on those identified areas. In schools, the regular evaluation of progress toward the campus vision and goals can be developed into a process of continuous improvement. However, campus leaders must focus on both the strengths and weaknesses of the campus in this process. Deficient areas can be improved to perform to standard, while areas performing at standard can be innovated for improvement.

117. B: Goal progress should be communicated effectively and in a timely manner, especially to those who are instrumental in achieving the goal. The school leader should communicate progress toward a goal, whether positive or negative. When there is regression in progress or a lack of progress, two-way communication should occur with appropriate stakeholders to determine what unexpected barriers and challenges to accomplishing the goal need to be addressed. Communicating regression in progress toward a goal is necessary so that corrections can be made.

118. B: Creating an advisory committee and meeting with the committee regularly demonstrates that the leader is willing to hear other perspectives and opinions prior to making decisions. A school leader may believe one course of action is correct but then change their mind after receiving feedback from an advisory committee. A school leader can demonstrate a willingness to change by getting information from a variety of sources prior to making decisions.

119. D: A leader should frequently communicate with parents and the community about progress toward goals in a variety of ways. This can include community meetings, but communication should not be limited to in-person meetings. The leader can provide a newsletter or bulletin that will update the community about school performance, upcoming events, and ways to get involved with the school to help achieve the school goals. Many schools feature phone systems that can mass call students' homes, which can be used to communicate announcements regarding school goals and progress toward those goals. Similarly, school leaders can mail letters to parents containing updates regarding the school goals.

120. C: The campus technology plan will include information such as when the computers were purchased, how they should be maintained, and when the computers should be replaced. If it is time to replace the computers, the school leader needs to identify what funds in the budget can be used to purchase new computers. If it is not time to replace the computers, the school leader may request technical support for improving the functionality of the computers.

Constructed Response

1. Essay question graders commonly look for the following elements in a strong response: strong content knowledge, clear organization, and effective arguments or examples. Language and usage are not usually strictly graded, but they can make a big impact on the clarity of your ideas.

Please use the provided rubric to make sure your response meets these common criteria. Try to have a friend or family member grade your response for you or take a break after writing your response and return to grade it with fresh eyes.

CONSTRUCTED RESPONSE RUBRIC

Domain	Description
Content Knowledge	• The response directly addresses every part of the prompt. • The response demonstrates independent knowledge of the topic. • The response discusses the topic at an appropriate depth.
Organization	• The response introduces the topic, usually with a thesis statement or by restating the prompt. • The response directly addresses the prompt by providing a clear and concise answer or solution. • The answer or solution is supported by logical arguments or evidence. • The response restates the main idea in the conclusion.
Arguments and Examples	• The response provides a reasonable answer to the prompt. • The answer is supported by strong reasoning or evidence. • The response develops ideas logically and connects ideas to one another. • The reasoning and evidence provided act to support a unified main idea.
Language and Usage	• The response demonstrates effective use of grammar and uses varied sentence structure throughout the response. • The response demonstrates correct use of spelling, punctuation, and capitalization. • The response demonstrates strong and varied use of vocabulary relevant to the topic and appropriate for the intended audience.

2. Essay question graders commonly look for the following elements in a strong response: strong content knowledge, clear organization, and effective arguments or examples. Language and usage are not usually strictly graded, but they can make a big impact on the clarity of your ideas.

Please use the provided rubric to make sure your response meets these common criteria. Try to have a friend or family member grade your response for you or take a break after writing your response and return to grade it with fresh eyes.

Constructed Response Rubric

Domain	Description
Content Knowledge	• The response directly addresses every part of the prompt. • The response demonstrates independent knowledge of the topic. • The response discusses the topic at an appropriate depth.
Organization	• The response introduces the topic, usually with a thesis statement or by restating the prompt. • The response directly addresses the prompt by providing a clear and concise answer or solution. • The answer or solution is supported by logical arguments or evidence. • The response restates the main idea in the conclusion.
Arguments and Examples	• The response provides a reasonable answer to the prompt. • The answer is supported by strong reasoning or evidence. • The response develops ideas logically and connects ideas to one another. • The reasoning and evidence provided act to support a unified main idea.
Language and Usage	• The response demonstrates effective use of grammar and uses varied sentence structure throughout the response. • The response demonstrates correct use of spelling, punctuation, and capitalization. • The response demonstrates strong and varied use of vocabulary relevant to the topic and appropriate for the intended audience.

3. Essay question graders commonly look for the following elements in a strong response: strong content knowledge, clear organization, and effective arguments or examples. Language and usage are not usually strictly graded, but they can make a big impact on the clarity of your ideas.

Please use the provided rubric to make sure your response meets these common criteria. Try to have a friend or family member grade your response for you or take a break after writing your response and return to grade it with fresh eyes.

Constructed Response Rubric

Domain	Description
Content Knowledge	• The response directly addresses every part of the prompt. • The response demonstrates independent knowledge of the topic. • The response discusses the topic at an appropriate depth.
Organization	• The response introduces the topic, usually with a thesis statement or by restating the prompt. • The response directly addresses the prompt by providing a clear and concise answer or solution. • The answer or solution is supported by logical arguments or evidence. • The response restates the main idea in the conclusion.
Arguments and Examples	• The response provides a reasonable answer to the prompt. • The answer is supported by strong reasoning or evidence. • The response develops ideas logically and connects ideas to one another. • The reasoning and evidence provided act to support a unified main idea.
Language and Usage	• The response demonstrates effective use of grammar and uses varied sentence structure throughout the response. • The response demonstrates correct use of spelling, punctuation, and capitalization. • The response demonstrates strong and varied use of vocabulary relevant to the topic and appropriate for the intended audience.

4. Constructed response items will be scored holistically on a scale of 1-3 according to the following performance indicators:

Completion	The degree to which the examinee addresses all parts of the prompt
Relevancy/Analysis	The degree to which the examinee demonstrates understanding of and responds to the issues presented with sound strategies for resolution
Organization/Clarity	The degree to which the examinee presents their response and supporting evidence in an organized, coherent manner
Use of supporting evidence	The degree to which the examinee supports their response and resolution strategies using specific, appropriate, and relevant examples and/or details
Language Use	The degree to which the examinee demonstrates competence in the use of language, including sentence variety, grammar, and mechanics

Examinees that receive an overall score of "3" demonstrate a high degree of competence in the following areas related to the assignment:

- All parts of the prompt are addressed with thoroughness and attention to detail
- The examinee demonstrates strong understanding of the issues presented
- The examinee responds to the issues presented with sound strategies for resolution
- Information in the response is very well-organized, clear, and accessible to the reader
- The examinee supports their response using ample specific, appropriate, and relevant examples and/or details
- The response is free of errors related to language usage, grammar, and mechanics